Secret Cotswolds

Secret Cotswolds

CROSS-STITCH DESIGNS INSPIRED BY THE WINDRUSH VALLEY

Lorna Bolingbroke

Black Sheep Press *of* **Oxford**

BLACK SHEEP PRESS of OXFORD LTD
P.O. BOX 722, Oxford OX2 6XR

Book Design by the M.A.Dhouse, Oxford
Printed in the U.K. by The Bath Press, Bath

ISBN 1 900232 02 2

Contents

Acknowledgements

So many people have helped me in the course of producing this book that I shall need another just to find the space to thank them! Perhaps the greatest thank–you should go to Stuart Birtwistle, the presiding genius at Black Sheep Press, who never once balked in the face of my various eccentricities and, for a man totally new to stitching, took the whole project on board in the most generous way imaginable. Of the other indefatigable employees at BSP, Alex Fuller deserves a special mention – I simply don't know anybody else who would have worked as hard as he did in order to get this book into print.   Neither can I leave out David Mitchell at The M.A.D.House who has made an invaluable contribution.

I cannot find the words to express a big enough recommendation for two Oxfordshire needlecraft suppliers who kept me sane throughout the entire exercise – Jan and David Cohen at Burford Needlecraft and Jill Budd at To the Point in Bicester. Their kindness and generosity are truly humbling and I only hope stitchers living in their areas realise how fortunate they are to have such wonderful people to help them. Similarly my framer, Ken Harmsworthy, is the sweetest man alive as well as being the best framer I have ever encountered, although Bill at Bill Posters in Witney also deserves a mention for helping me out of a tight spot.

On the technical side, I L Soft at Witney deserve praise both for their excellent product and for their immense patience with a total technophobe experiencing various hardware nightmares. Similarly I cannot imagine a more calming influence than Barry Roberts which is all the more incredible given that he works in the altogether fraught world of photography. I am continually amazed by his skill, not least in dealing with the foibles of primadonna felines such as Buster, Pusslie and Osbert!

I am entirely indebted to Mika who, I am sure everybody will agree, is more talented than anybody deserves to be. Her enthusiasm and immense patience put my poor efforts to shame.

I would also like to mention my "mum", Veronica Ashby, whose continual inventiveness, consummate expertise and inextinguishable sense of humour are a constant source of inspiration to her less talented offspring. Similarly I "owe" my friend, Henrietta Fife who is just what best friends should be – always at the end of the telephone when one wants to moan and the first at the front door with a bottle of wine when there is cause to celebrate. Christine Agg and her immense family also deserve a big thank you for keeping every disaster in perspective.

Lastly, I would like to issue a big hug to my stitching-hating husband who displayed more patience than I realised he possessed – it's OK now, John, you can put your "needlework face" away!

This book is dedicated, with humility and immense gratitude to "my ladies" who stitched most of the examples within:

Maristela Skrenski

Gill and Carol Henderson

Suzanne Esson

Phillippa Tomlinson

Patricia Curtis

Angela Taylor

Julie Short

Norah Hunt

Thanks girls, I couldn't have done it without you.

Introduction

Many people were amazed by the result of a recent survey which discovered that 70 % of the British population would prefer to live in the country. I did not feel that the outcome was that surprising: some indication of the strength of our fascination with the countryside and rural life in general may surely be found in the vast array of country-based publications on sale in the "general interest" section of any large newsagent! I like to think that attachment to "the land" is firmly embedded in our gene-pool – an echo of the days before enclosure and the Industrial Revolution made town existence the norm. Certainly the one feature of this country that many ex-pats miss the most is its green-ness (although I suspect they are grateful to escape the climate that creates it!), and I think it does us all good to see acres of English grassland with nothing higher than the bordering trees.

Obviously if all 70 % of the populace got their wish and discovered themselves residing in rural Britain they would be faced with the classic problem of the tourist-trap – the sheer numbers would destroy the very thing that they valued. I also question whether many of the people who say they would like to escape from the town have really thought the issue through: are they just seduced by the "roses around the door" image of the country? For example, it is rare indeed to find a supermarket and other shopping facilities within walking distance of one's village, and pizza delivery operations (unfortunately!) are virtually non-existent! On a hot summer's day I do not rate being stuck behind a manure-laden tractor as one of life's enriching experiences and however picturesque non-tarmacked tracks may be I defy anybody to enjoy the experience of having to negotiate one after days of downpour! That having been said, those of us fortunate enough to live in a rural area believe these occasional inconveniences are more than balanced by the sheer peace; the privilege of looking up at night-time to see the stars unobscured by street lighting, and, most importantly, the ability to enjoy life at a less than breakneck pace. Nor have I mentioned the country people who must surely rank amongst the best souls to walk the earth – sadly, how many town dwellers could say that about their neighbours?

Like it or not, out of necessity towns have to be populated. But I do question that in living in urban areas one has to turn one's back entirely on the traditions of country life. "Country fare" – the wonderful hams, breads, cakes, pastries and jams – are as tasty on the town table as on the farmhouse board and stitching too in its various forms is an important part of our heritage which is equally accessible in town or country. I firmly believe that in working our pieces of embroidery, quilting or cross stitch we are forming a bond with our forebears; preserving and even extending their tradition of fine needlework.

It is with this attitude that I approached this book. But, before everybody gets the impression that I am a frightfully worthy but somewhat po-faced mortal, I would like to stress that I am strongly in favour of Fun with a capital F and I don't think stitching should be excluded from this. After all, why spend time doing something if you don't enjoy it – life is simply too short! Despite the occasional disasters, I received a great deal of pleasure from developing the designs found in this book and I would be desperately sorry to think that any of my designs were being stitched out of a sense of necessity rather than self-indulgence.

As the discerning reader may have gathered, I am fortunate enough to live in the Cotswolds (well, at least on the edge of them!) and I feel passionately proud and protective of the area in general. I also believe that this part of the country holds a special place in the nation's consciousness, although I would not dream of suggesting that the Cotswolds are "better" than, for example, the Dales and the Peaks. Rather they are like different members of the same family and we love them equally for their differences. To me, the Cotswolds are like an old friend with whom one is absolutely at one's ease, they are comfortable and "lived-in" and I know many people I have spoken to in this vein feel the same way.

However, I am concerned that many people visit this part of the world and only see a tiny fraction of the riches it has to offer. How many people "do" the Cotswolds and only see its public face at Burford, Stow-on-the-Wold or Bourton-on-the-Water, not realising that there are sights more breathtaking than these, lovely though they are? If through this book I can encourage even one person away from the allure of the more famous parts of the area and into exploration of the other "secret" 90% I will feel entirely vindicated. Or perhaps I am being self-indulgent and expecting people to enjoy careering down single track roads in search of adventure in the same way I do?!

Primarily this book is called "Secret Cotswolds" because its designs are taken from interesting but under-visited spots. In the course of producing it, it occurred to me that if any of my readers are as inveterately nosy as I am they will want to know exactly from where the inspiration comes, and, because I have also been known to enjoy teasing, I'm not going to tell! However, I have included clues of varying degrees of crypticism for the more tenacious puzzler to tackle should they accept the challenge and happen to be in the area to undertake the necessary research. I would gain an immense amount of pleasure from receiving readers' solutions to the puzzles should anybody wish to forward their guesses to me – but I cannot guarantee to reveal the answers!

About the designs

The keen-eyed reader will notice that there are no drainpipes etc. on my designs and might imagine that everybody in the Cotswolds enjoys being flooded. Obviously this is not the case and I can assure everybody that drainpipes are alive and well and living in Oxfordshire! I must stress that all my designs are based on real places and not replicas of them. I fail to see the aesthetic joys of drainpipes, municipal waste bins and the odd shed and have therefore missed them out. If anybody really wants a warts-and-all version of any of my designs I should be delighted to supply them with one – you have been warned though! Similarly, on occasions I have allowed myself a free rein with, in particular, gardens – although I would argue that I am doing nothing more or less than a good gardener does in selecting plants of varying hues to grow for the next season. In any case my "fiddlings" add to the excitement of trying to work out the real location!

I am of the opinion that cross stitchers are in the main either "Anchor-people" or "DMC-people". Unpatriotically, I am of the latter breed simply because my mother and grandmother, who taught me how to sew, are too. Bearing this in mind I tend to design with the DMC palettes in my upper consciousness and thus all the examples included in this book have been stitched using DMC threads. I entirely understand that "Anchor-people" will tend to have Anchor threads already and therefore I have supplied conversion charts for them. However, they will achieve slightly different results and I would be interested to see any Anchor-based projects if anybody would like to send me a photograph (I'll try to return any, although obviously I cannot make any promises). I'm not making a value-judgement DMC-versus-Anchor – as I am at pains to state in the "how to..." section, one's choice of threads, like choice of material, method and colour, is a personal thing and neither better nor worse than anybody else's.

Similarly, in the course of stitching my designs, my "ladies" have independently commented that I do use more than the usual number of colours. I make no apologies for this – as I do not use either fractional stitches or much backstitch there has to be a compensation somewhere and my designs need careful shading to achieve the depth at which I aim. However, I would say that in most instances there is a very easy way around this "problem" and that is to substitute colours you already have in your workbox. This is particularly appropriate with regard to flowers – as mentioned above, in most cases I have already "fiddled" and your own substitutions (as long as they are not too extensive) are not going to ruin the design. I cannot stress enough that I am not the "design-police" and I am actually rather excited by the idea of my ideas being altered to create new works. So please don't worry if you really like pink flowers and in the design I have selected yellow – experiment and enjoy the chance to be creative – you'll be producing your own unique piece! Again I would be delighted to see any adaptations you are particularly proud of if you would take the trouble to contact me; if I have learnt anything from stitching it is that it is a good thing to share and that none or us are so clever that we cannot learn from others. Perhaps that is the best thing about the pastime – it's a great leveller!

The last words – enjoy your stitching!

A Note on the Charts

Since the pattern charts are too large to fit on one page, an overlap has been provided to help match one section with the next. These overlaps extend to 5 squares, and are highlighted on the charts by a grey stripe as in the example below. To help you further, there is a page layout diagram before each chart illustrating how the different parts of the chart fit together.

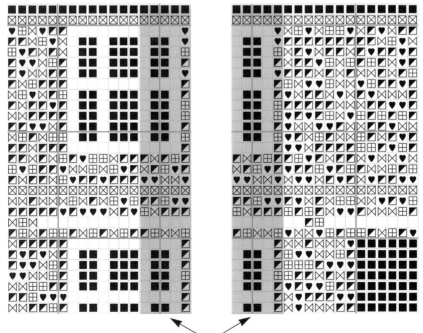

The 5 last squares of the chart edge
are repeated on the next page.

Cross Stitch and how to do it

As one might guess from the name "cross stitch" the point of the exercise is to make a stitch on the fabric that in close up looks like a little cross. My designs are built up from many such stitches worked in different colours which together form a blended whole. As far as embroidery stitches go, few are easier to learn or to get good results with quickly than cross stitch. The basic starting point is the chart and you will see that these are composed of symbols sitting inside grid squares. **Don't worry if initially you find the charts quite daunting** – I can assure you that after only a very short time you'll be confidently skipping through even the largest of them! Each chart symbol has a colour associated with it which is listed in an accompanying key. For each symbol you should make a cross stitch in that colour.

To make the stitches there are two methods and I don't think it matters which one you use: after all stitching is meant to be an enjoyable experience and the most important thing is that you are comfortable with whatever method you follow. However, for the purists, I would mention that there is a tiny difference in the stitch produced by each method so if you are a perfectionist it might be an idea to stick to one or the other. Pragmatists, such as myself, weigh up the virtually unnoticeable difference in appearance against ease of working and mix the two methods quite happily. Again, I am keen not to make a judgement one way or the other – it's entirely up to personal preference!

The first method involves making whole individual stitches one by one. If you look at Diagram 1 on the next page this will help you get to grips with this technique. If you bring your needle up through the fabric at point 1; push it back through at point 2; bring it up again at point 3 and finally back down at point 4 you will have made one whole cross-stitch. Assuming another stitch in the same colour is required next door to this one if you bring your needle up again at point 3; down at point 5, up at point 6 and down at point 2 you will now have two cross stitches sitting side by side. And so on..!

The second method I find particularly useful if a long row of stitches of the same colour is required. Instead of forming single whole stitches one at a time you work a row of half stitches and go back over them filling in the top crosses. Diagram 2 explains this method: bring your needle up through the fabric at point 1; put it back down through point 6; up again at 3, down at 4, up at 5 and down at 2. You will now have a row of "half-stitches". To fill in the top crosses, bring the needle up at point 7, down at point 4; up at 5; down at two; up at 3 and down at 8. You will now have three full cross stitches sitting side by side.

That is essentially how cross stitch works and I am sure anybody will agree that it is very easy! The most important thing to remember is that **all the "top" stitches should point the same way** as it creates an even effect. Again I am adamant that it does not matter if yours point top-right-to-bottom-left or top-left-to-bottom-right as long as you are happy with the result.

My designs do not use any "fractional stitches" so I will not waste time and paper by describing how to work these. Suffice it to say that although the use of these stitches does give one more scope in terms of design, they are usually fiddly to work and almost universally loathed by stitchers, myself included. From a design point of view also they can be a mixed blessing as injudicious use can create an uneven effect. If you get into cross stitch through this book and want to learn more about different techniques such as fractional stitches, I strongly recommend you purchase one of the excellent magazines currently on the market. These usually have comprehensive instructions on various techniques and graded examples for you to try out. They are also a relatively inexpensive way to develop your skills.

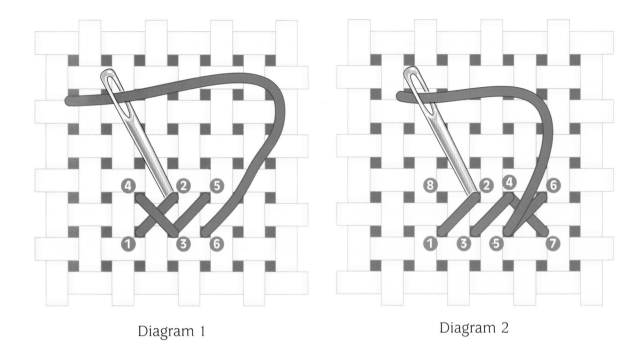

Diagram 1   Diagram 2

Fabrics and threads

I believe I am safe in saying that most cross stitchers use Aida fabric. This is a specialist cross stitch fabric having clearly visible "holes", making it easy to work with even in less than perfectly lit rooms. It comes in different "counts", enabling one to work a different number of stitches to the inch. The most commonly used count is 14 and, as aforementioned, all the examples in this book are worked on this count. However, I do think many of my designs would look good on 18 count and if anybody is keen to try this I would be very interested to see the results.

The other fabric possibility is evenweave which also has "counts"; however these are usually much higher in number than Aida because a cross stitch is worked over two threads of fabric. Thus 28 count evenweave equates to 14 count Aida, 36 count evenweave to 18 count Aida and so on. Many cross stitchers do not like working with evenweave because of the added difficulty resulting from the necessity of working over two threads and again I do not take a hard line on this – whatever you are happy and comfortable with is right! However, I would add that evenweave is much easier to use if you are contemplating working a design with many fractional stitches.

With regard to colour of fabric I do not recommend bright white Aida as I think this would be too harsh for my designs. The examples used in this book have been worked in Antique White which is a far softer effect. In most cases this has meant that I have worked stitches to represent "sky": for those who want to keep the number of stitches worked to a minimum I suggest working the entire design on sky blue fabric and missing out the "sky" stitches. This will create roughly the same effect as working the actual stitches but will mean that the Aida "holes" will be more visible – the choice is yours!

All the examples have been worked with DMC thread. We have supplied Anchor alternatives for those who prefer to use these but the results will not be completely identical. Both Anchor and DMC thread is supplied in 8 metre skeins and the thread is divisible into six separate strands. If you work with 14 count Aida (or 28 count evenweave) the convention is to separate out two of these strands to form a thinner "working thread". This is what the oft-written instruction "work with two threads of DMC/Anchor" means. In the case of 18 count Aida the convention is to use just one strand which, in conjunction with the finer count fabric, creates a finer texture. As mentioned above, I think that many of my designs would suit the 18 count/single strand treatment and I would be delighted to hear from anybody who works with this

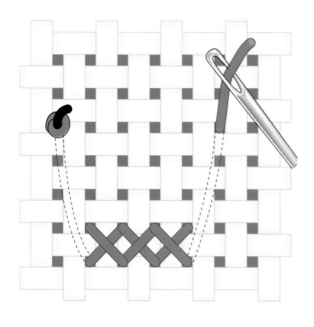 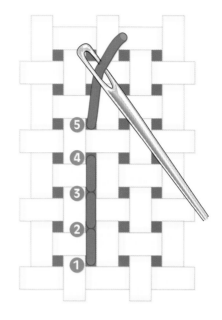

Diagram 3   Diagram 4

specification. The sharp eyed amongst you will note that the same colour might have different descriptions from one chart to another: this is because colour is relative and whilst it might be correct to designate a colour "light grey" in one situation it would be entirely inappropriate description in another.

With regard to fabric and thread I cannot stress enough that **you should use the best quality of materials you can afford**. Unfortunately with stitching as with much else you only get what you pay for and, bearing in mind the hours you are likely to spend working a project, it would be sad to achieve a substandard result through skimping on materials.

Starting to work your design

Whatever fabric you use I recommend that you curb your impatience to begin stitching and lightly hem the cut edges before you begin! It does make life easier in the long run as frays from unfinished edges are very quick to find their way into the back of your work and make a mess of what might have otherwise been a neat result. (It also prevents the material "evaporating" and potentially leaving you with too small a piece of material to finish the design!). With regard to size of fabric I am inclined to be generous and allow at least 5cm more fabric than you need all the way round the design (I usually make it 10cm to be absolutely on the safe side but some would say this is pure paranoia!).

I strongly recommend that you start from the middle of the design and work outwards as this ensures that the work is centred correctly on the fabric. It would be tragic to spend many hours working a design from the top downwards only to find that you had miscalculated and did not have enough material to complete the design. We have indicated the middle squares of each design by slightly greying that square and this is where you should begin stitching. With regard to your fabric, the easiest method of finding the centre is to fold the fabric in half each way and lightly press the fold – the point at which the fold lines cross will be the centre. Alternatively, if you are using Aida fabric, you could count the number of squares and divide by two.

When working with stranded cotton and Aida/evenweave you should really use a hoop or frame as this keeps the tension of your stitches even. Some stitchers like to crank up the tension until it is absolutely drum-tight, others keep it slack-but even – again, the choice is yours!

When making your first stitch the easiest way of casting on is to knot the thread and push the needle in about 2cm away from where you intend to begin stitching. Bring the thread up at the correct place for the first stitch and work the stitches for that colour thread as indicated on the chart. When you have worked up to the point where the knot appears, simply snip it off – the stitches you have made will hold the thread at the back of the work and effectively weave it into the fabric of your stitching. Similarly, when you have exhausted that length of thread, work your last stitch leaving the needle at the back of the fabric and then push it up a few centimetres away. As you work more stitches this left-over thread will be held in place, leaving no loose untidy ends. Diagram 3 shows these techniques. Alternatively, you can weave starting and finishing threads into the back of your work to create a neat appearance but you should never leave any knots behind your work as they create a bumpy unpleasant effect when your finished work is framed.

I have tried to keep backstitch details to a minimum but where these do appear you should work them only when all the cross stitches have been completed. Diagram 4 shows how to back stitch: bring your needle up through the fabric at point 1, down again at point 2, up again at 3, down at 2, up at 4, down at 3, up at 5 and so on. Usually back stitch is worked in the same number of threads as the cross stitches: two with 14 count Aida, one with 18 count Aida etc. As all the photographed designs in the book are worked on 14 count Aida with two strands, the backstitch has similarly been worked in two strands unless otherwise indicated.

Cleaning, stretching and framing

Once your design has been completed of course you will want to display it to its best advantage and framing is the convention. That having been said, I would be delighted to hear from anybody who uses my designs in more unusual situations! However, before you can even think about framing your picture you should really wash your design as, no matter how clean your hands are, grease from them does get into the threads and fabric as you work (not to mention, if you are anything like me, debris from the numerous chocolate biscuits consumed during my stitching periods!). Some people get very worried at the thought of washing their work but it is really no problem if you follow some basic rules.

- Always hand wash. Although one of my great-aunts puts her embroideries in a pillowcase and then in her washing machine on a gentle cycle with, to date, no adverse results, this is a convenience too far for me!

- Try to use warmish, but not hot, water for the actual wash and rinse with cold. I find that the shower attachment on my bath taps is a great way to rid my work of soap, otherwise simple rinsing under the tap is quite in order.

- With regard to soap powder, try to use either specialist needlecraft brands (available at most needlecraft shops) or powders/liquids designed for wool or delicate fabrics. Ordinary washing powders are not recommended as most do contain chemicals which affect the colour of the washed items.

- Try not to rub at the stitches as this can roughen them and create an uneven effect when they dry out.

- Wring very gently to get as much water as possible out of the work. People watching me do this usually experience a sharp intake of breath at this point but if you have worked the piece in the manner described above it will be well able to take this treatment.

- Dry the piece flat after teasing it back gently into shape – you should not completely dry the work but leave it just slightly damp.

- Iron on the wrong side of the work with the hottest iron the fabric can take. It helps if you put a fluffy towel underneath the embroidery as this cushions the work allowing the stitches to stand out properly. Steam is not recommended (if, as above, the work is slightly damp you won't need it anyway) but work the point of the iron into the stitches. **Never** iron the top of the stitches as this flattens them and creates a most odd effect.

- Don't fold your work once it has been ironed but roll it round something – the insides of toilet rolls or kitchen paper rolls are ideal.

Don't panic if you a colour starts to run. Just turn the tap onto cold and run water through the work until the colour bleed stops – it always does! This should also prevent the colour bleeding permanently into the surrounding fabric.

You are now ready to think about framing. Cross stitch doesn't distort as much as some other textures but usually some stretching improves the appearance. Some magazines and other books suggest you try this yourself but I always find that a good framer can achieve far better results than I can and the price is usually included in the cost of framing. After all, you have made something which will, hopefully, last for many years so I take the view that it is worth asking a professional to deal with this side of the process. Similarly, good framers will also lace your work onto backing board and I again I recommend you ask yours to do this for you: whenever I have tried DIY-lacing I have experienced "three month sag" and have ended up taking the work back to my framer so I have to ask myself was it worth the effort?! If you can't find a framer who will undertake these processes on your behalf make enquiries at your local needlecraft shop who I invariably find are a mine of information and more than happy to help you.

All the examples included in this book have been double-mounted which means that two colours have been used to make up the mount. I found that this brought out the depth in the designs – but if you prefer single, or even want to try triple mounts the choice is yours. I would be interested to see some of the results if anybody is particularly pleased with theirs. Choosing the mount(s) is something which needs time – I and my colleagues played for hours before making our decisions and a good framer will take the time and trouble to make sure that the end result is both pleasing to you and grateful to the design. Even the width of mount used can affect the look of a design. Similarly, the choice of frames on the market is huge and merely changing the style of frame used can alter the whole tone of your work. Don't worry if you do take an age choosing the right setting, as I mentioned earlier you are going to have to live with the result for a long time and it is important to get it right.

The issue of glass or no-glass is hotly debated in stitching circles and I come down on the side of using glass purely for the sake of convenience. Personally I cannot see the point of going to all the trouble of cleaning, stretching and framing your work only to have to go through the process all over again when it gets grubby (as it invariably does even in the cleanest house when hung without glass for any length of time). I also think, probably incorrectly, that glass protects your work from the elements! Having said that, if you really want to frame without glass it is entirely up to you and there are arguments for doing so, the most notable being that you retain the "real" colour of the work and are able to see the stitches more clearly. As with many other issues in connection with stitching, it comes down to personal preference and whatever gives you the most pleasure. The most important thing is that you enjoy doing the work and enjoy the finished result.

Part 1

The Upper Windrush Valley

The Upper Windrush Valley

The village of Naunton is a definitive example of what people imagine when they talk about a "Cotswold village". Nestling amongst the gently rolling hills it is spread out along the banks of the Windrush which at this stage is quite a small river. I find the large number of water pumps particularly fascinating and can easily imagine the picturesque scenes in days gone by as villagers queued to draw water. There is also an extremely unusual (and enormous!) stone dovecote which excites one's curiosity – who on earth would want to keep that many doves and house them in such splendour?

My especially favourite place in Naunton is the Black Horse Inn which is a wonderful place from which to start a walk and a delight to sit in after having completed one. However, my comfort is not the only point of interest, as there is a possibility that the Black Horse of the title refers to the horses ridden by King Arthur's knights patrolling their territorial border in this area. Being an incurable romantic I find my thoughts wandering towards the distant age of chivalry and the Celtic Golden Age every time I visit this pub.

As there are so many opportunities for walks around Naunton I am not going to discuss any in particular as it would find it too cruel to have to make a choice of which ones to cover and unfortunately space does not permit my listing them all. I will therefore restrict myself to recommending the Wardens' Way and the Windrush Way, both of which take in some stunning countryside and also have the benefit of being extremely well signposted.

The piquantly titled Upper and Lower Slaughters are well worth a visit, if only for their name! Despite the images of bloodshed this conjures up, none of the attempts at explaining its origin include any gore or fighting. One school of thought thinks it may refer to the ancient profusion of sloe trees in this area and another, less romantically, to muddy puddles! Yet a third opinion beleives the name stems from the Norman knight d'Scholtres, who erected a castle next to the Norman church. What is certain is that by the sixteenth century there was a family answering to the name of Slaughter installed in the area, whether by accident or through assimilation I do not know. In the more recent past the famous architect Sir Edwin Lutyens restored some of the cottages at Upper Slaughter whilst the church at Lower Slaughter has a fibreglass spire-top following restoration in the late 1960s. (I have not attempted to centre a design around this!).The watermill at Lower Slaughter is also well worth a visit.

The Swells are another strangely-named collection of villages and, no, they do not refer to the state of my waistline after I have visited all my favourite pubs and teashops! A chalybeate spring, discovered in the early nineteenth century, prompted speculation regarding the development of a spa to rival Leamington and Harrogate. Fortunately for the peace of the area, if not the local economy, the plan failed and the village of Lowe Swell remains as picturesque as ever.

Another place which every traveller must visit is Winchcombe, which has had a turbulent past. The first sign of habitation in this area is the impressive New Stone Age long barrow Belas Knap and nothing much seems to have happened until the Romans turned up about 2,000 years later. In Saxon times Winchcombe was the seat of one of the kings of Mercia The nunnery and abbey originally founded by King Offa and King Caenwulf respectively and rebuilt following a Danish invasion ensured the prosperity of the town as pilgrims came to visit the shrine of the murdered boy-king St Kenelm. The parish church of St Peter built in the perpendicular style has particularly grotesque gargoyles sometimes called the "Winchcombe Worthies" and legend has it these caricature the monks from the abbey, who were not popular in the town. Following the Dissolution Winchcombe was plunged into commercial decline from which it never really recovered, in contrast to the prosperous Cotswold wool towns whose glory days were just beginning. There was an experiment with tobacco growing but the government made this activity illegal in 1640 to protect the economy of Virginia and despite a riot in protest against this measure, little commercial industry has flourished since that time.

There is so much in this area I could include that I could fill this book just with text! So I shall have to curb my enthusiasm and lead into the designs taken from the upper Windrush Valley.

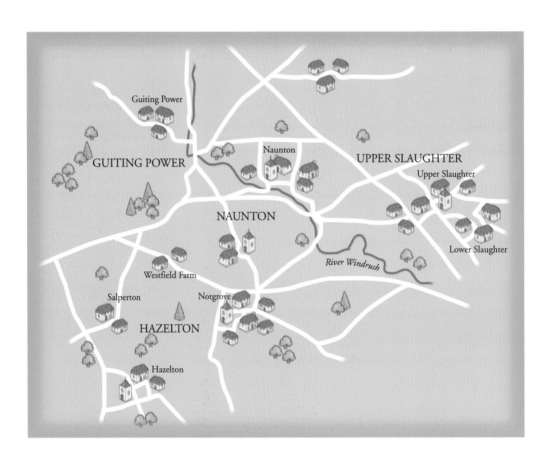

The Village Green

The title should give you the biggest clue to this cottage's whereabouts! I simply could not resist the combination of classic cottage windows with the slightly Gothic aperture above the door. Although in a busy place in this village it has a peaceful quality which I find very soothing, that is, when not consumed by curiosity regarding what lies behind the door!

Clue: On the way to goodness!

The Village Green

Page Layout:

22	23	24

Stitch Count: 120 x 86

Key

Cross stitch in two strands

		DMC	Anchor
△	Light Raspberry	316	60
9	Raspberry	3726	1018
P	Stone Grey	3022	1040
♠	Very Dark Moss Green	934	862
⊞	Moss Green	936	846
M	Dark Grass Green	469	267
►	Dark Forest Green	895	269
✳	Forest Green	3345	268
⊓	Dark Brown Stone	381	1008
+	Light Forest Green	3346	257
□	Mid Stone	382	391
⌐	Very Pale Sky Blue	3753	1031
⊥	Mid Moss Green	937	268
⊘	Dark Stone	3032	392
·	Light Stone	3033	387
−	Light Beige	613	853
⊡	Dark Slate	3787	10
★	Dove Grey	3023	832
◇	Pale Honey	738	942
●	Dark Chocolate Brown	3371	382
❚	Mid Brown	611	832
◥	Very Pale Grey	762	234
◸	Pale Grey	415	398
←	Grass Green	470	266
⊠	Dark Brown	610	889
━	Mid Green-Grey	367	216
⚏	Jade	320	215
=	Steel Grey	647	397
	White	Blanc	2
■	Black	310	403

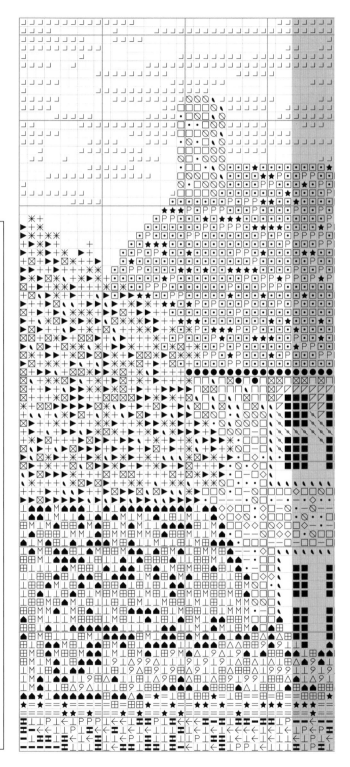

continued on p.24

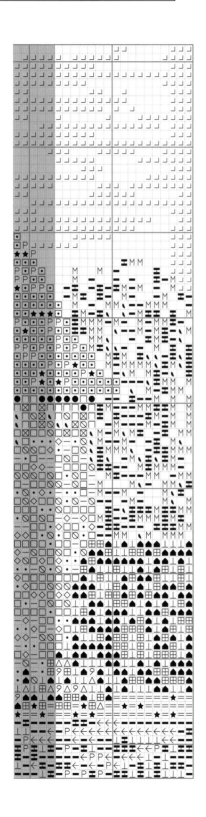

The Potting Shed

I am not entirely sure whether this building is put to use in the manner suggested by the title but my imagination was entirely captured by the idea of potting on one's seedlings in such an environment so I included it anyway. The structure of steps leading up to a raised door is quite common in this part of the world and always looks very cosmopolitan to me. Perhaps you could think up your own "use" for the building!

Clue: Yet more travel on the straight and narrow.

The Potting Shed

Page Layout:

26	27

Stitch Count: 90 x 100

Key

Cross stitch in two strands

		DMC	Anchor
■	Black	310	403
╲	Light Steel Grey	415	398
	White	Blanc	2
⊡	Dark Slate	3787	10
↓	Pale Terracotta	3828	373
⊘	Dark Stone	3032	392
╲	Honey	437	362
○	Light Stone	3033	387
⊠	Dark Brown	610	889
▶	Dark Forest Green	895	269
☰	Forest Green	3345	268
╲	Yellow Green	472	264
−	Very Pale Grey	762	234
+	Bright Grass Green	470	266
●	Dark Rose Pink	223	895
△	Rose Pink	224	894
▲	Very Dark Moss Green	934	862
▬	Moss Green	936	846
⊥	Mid Moss Green	937	268
◢	Very Dark Slate	3021	273
M	Dark Grass Green	469	267
▢	Mid Stone	3782	391
⊒	Mid Brown	611	832
⌐	Very Pale Sky Blue	3753	1031

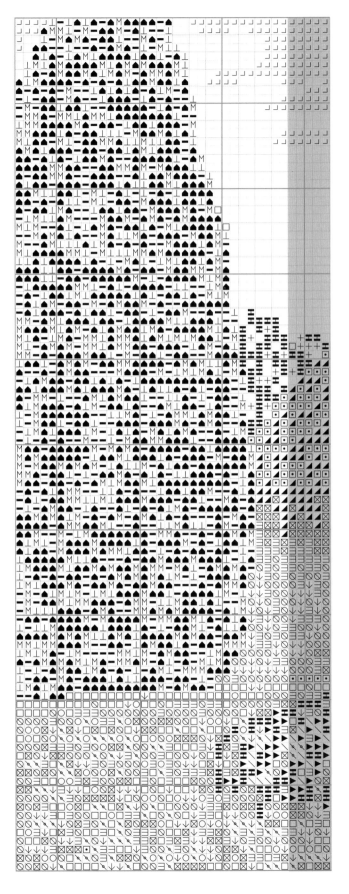

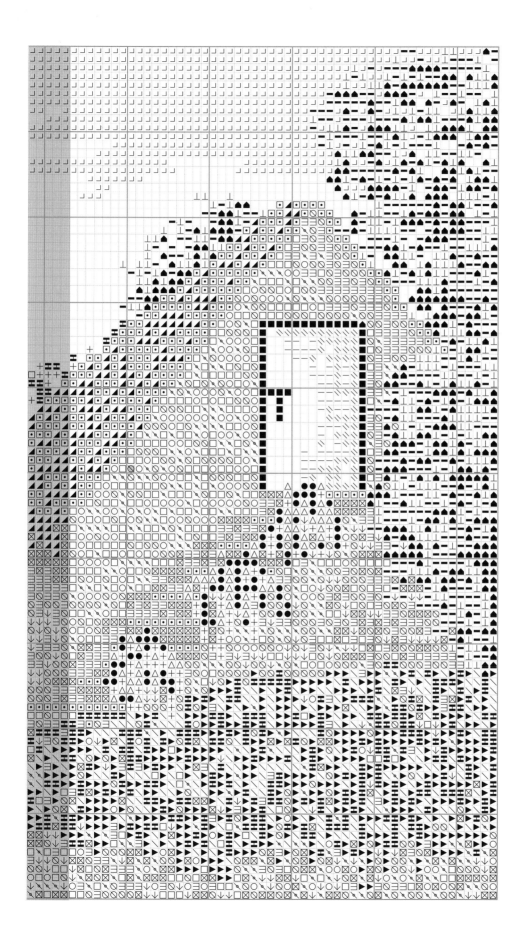

The Post Office

One of my relatives argues that you can have a truly thriving village only when it possesses a pub, a post office and a church (not necessarily listed in order of importance!). Certainly in my experience in all three there is no lack of talk, whether it's to catch up on the news, exchange views or canvas opinions on the issues important to the community at large. Sadly we are losing many of our village post offices-cum-shops and I think village society diminishes as a result. I have therefore tried to capture this one in all its glory and I hope you will be encouraged to not only stitch this as a tribute to a great British institution but also to call in to village shops when passing – use them or lose them!

Clue: Falls between temple and family.

Page Layout:

30	31	32
34	35	36

Key

Cross stitch in two strands   Stitch Count: 200 x 156

		DMC	Anchor			DMC	Anchor
☐	White	Blanc	2	−	Bright Gold	444	291
▽	Dark Pine Green	502	876	▬	Lovat	367	216
◇	Pale Honey	738	942	·	Grey	647	397
◀	Light Bottle Green	319	217	،	Mid Brown	611	832
T	Pillar Box Red	347	1025	+	Light Blue-Grey	3072	234
⊓	Parrot Green	986	245	☐	Mid Stone	3782	391
/	Pale Rose Pink	225	892	◪	Pale Lavender	3042	870
◁	Dark Steel Grey	535	1041	◆	Honey	437	362
H	Pine Green	503	875	⊡	Dark Slate	3787	10
⊍	Pale Terracotta	3828	373	♥	Stone Grey	3022	1040
△	Rose Pink	224	894	⬉	Very Light Stone	822	390
⫽	Very Dark Slate	3021	273	M	Dark Grass Green	469	267
○	Lavender	3041	871	⊥	Mid Moss Green	937	268
▼	Dark Red	815	1005	⟍	Mid Beige	612	831
⌐	Very Pale Sky Blue	3753	1031	\	Light Dove Grey	3024	899
☆	Light Stone	3033	387	■	Black	310	403
☰	Mid Grey	646	8581	✳	Light Beige	613	853
◤	Dark Moss Green	935	263	←	Bright Grass Green	470	266
⦸	Dark Stone	3032	392	⊠	Dark Brown	610	889
♡	Dove Grey	3023	832				

Backstitch in two strands

		DMC	Anchor
—	Black	310	403

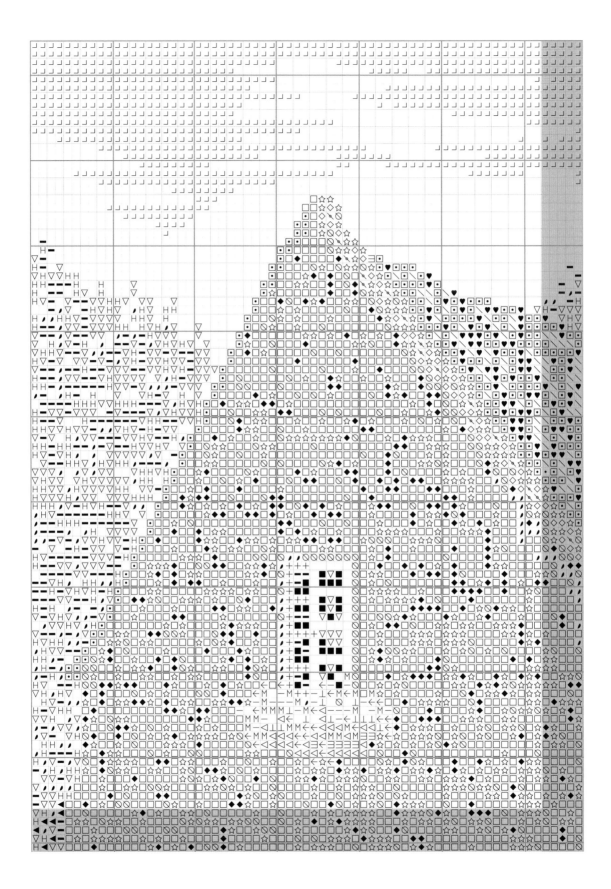

continued on p. 32

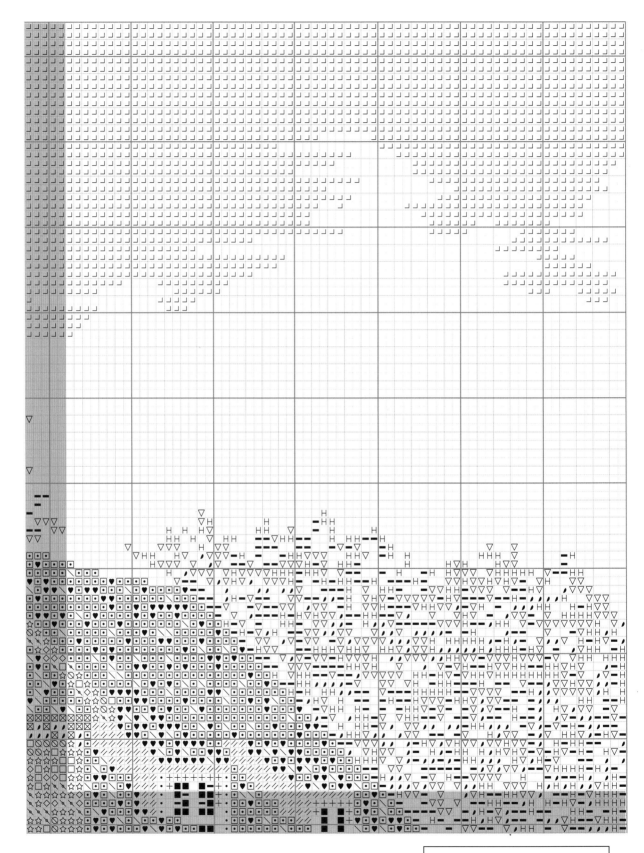

continued on p. 34

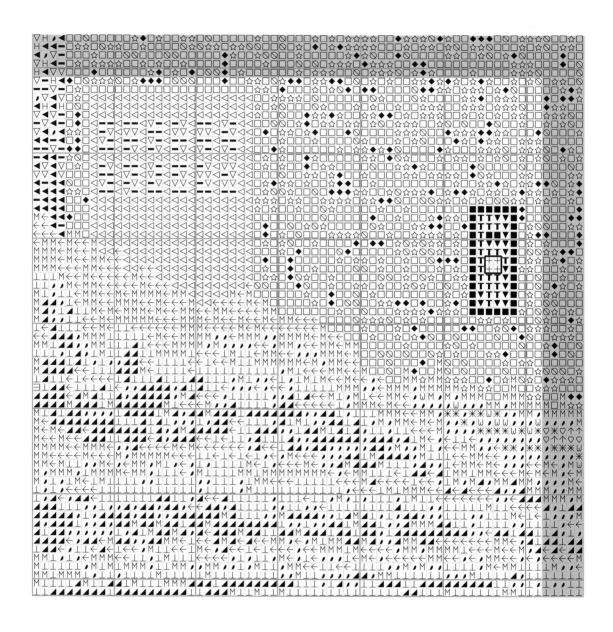

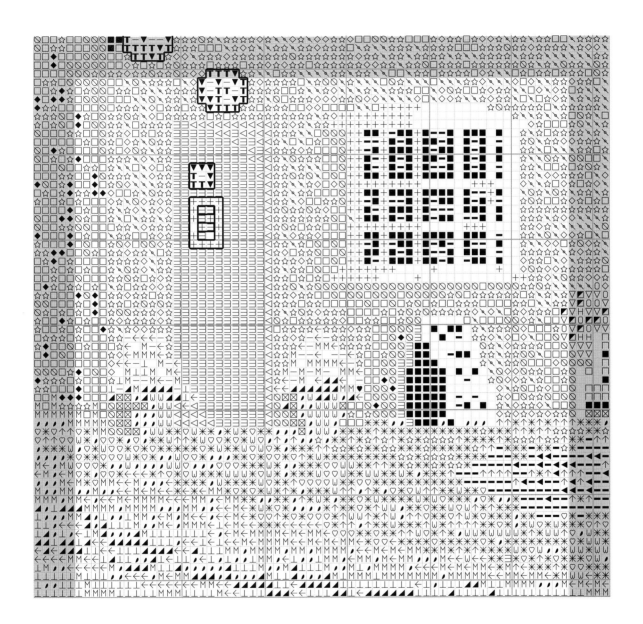

continued on p. 36

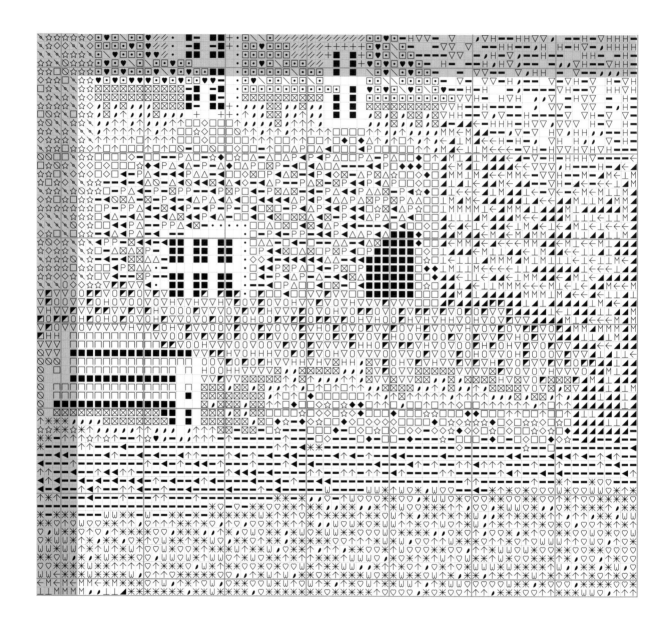

The Gate

This structure I find truly amazing not least because it may be found in the middle of nowhere up a single track road. I have no idea why such an imposing form should be so placed where only few can admire it but I am glad that stumbled across it and its nearby companion which unfortunately did not make it into this book! Although I am totally ignorant of its history I suspect that it may have been cobbled together from remnants of an ecclesiastical building as the tympanum over the door reminds me of many a church entrance. If this is the case it is tribute indeed to the ingenuity our forebears in making something beautiful from leftovers and, indeed, an excellent example of early recycling!

Clue: Bonkers, but not conkers!

The Gate

Page Layout:

39	**40**
41	**42**

Stitch Count: 117 x 140

*Detail from the engraving
on a local gravestone*

Key

Cross stitch in two strands

		DMC	Anchor			DMC	Anchor
⊓	Amber	433	371	↖	Light Stone Pink	842	376
::	Pale Honey	738	942	◢	Dark Golden-Brown	869	906
⊿	Dark Chocolate Brown	3371	382	◁	Mid Stone Pink	841	378
◆	Dark Olive	3051	860	⊡	Pale Mink	642	831
⩘	Grass Green	320	215	⊥	Mid Moss Green	937	268
▬	Lovat	367	216	M	Dark Grass Green	469	267
▬	Very Light Stone Pink	543	933	⊘	Dark Stone	3032	392
▲	Very Dark Moss Green	934	862	⟍	Mid Beige	612	831
⊞	Very Dark Slate	3021	273	⊍	Pale Terracotta	3828	373
⊠	Dark Brown	610	889	☐	Mid Stone	3782	391
T	Pillar Box Red	347	1025	●	Mid Brown	611	832
⚌	Mid Green-Brown	3012	843				
★	Chocolate Brown	938	381				
⌐	Very Pale Sky Blue	3753	1031				
✳	Light Amber	434	365				

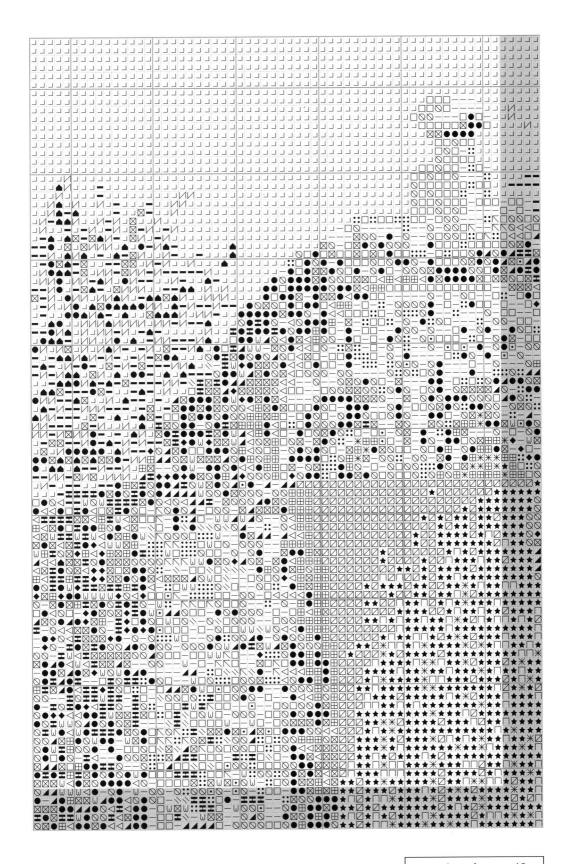

continued on p. 40

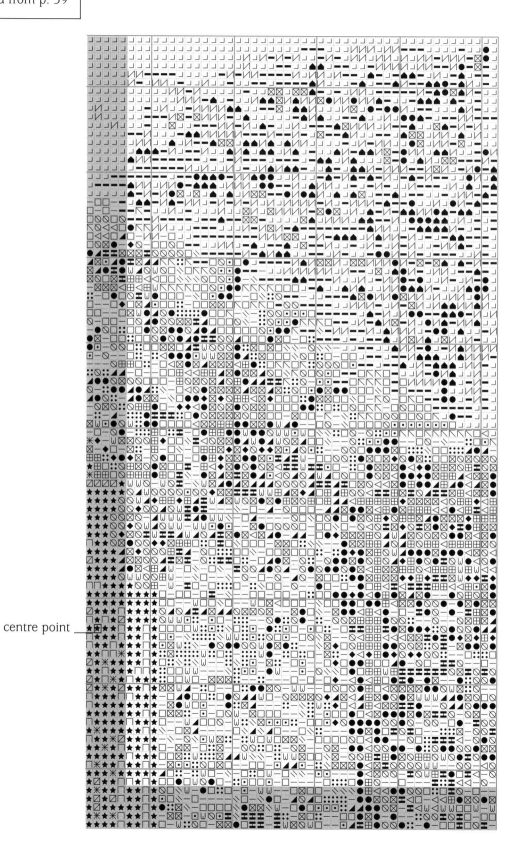

centre point

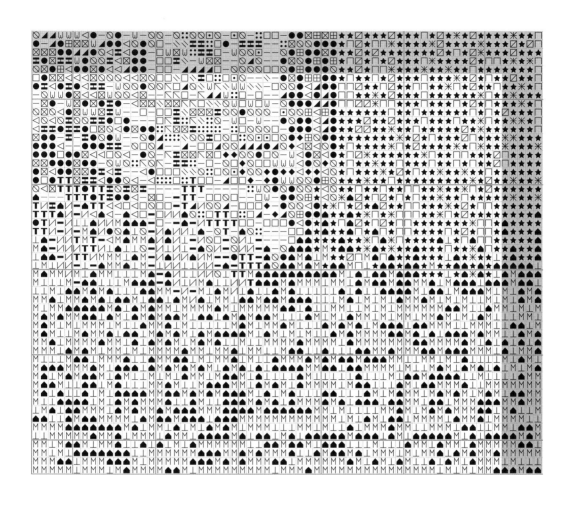

continued on p. 42

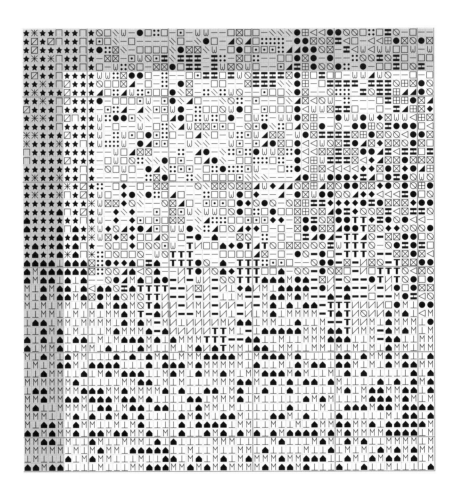

Part 2

The Middle Reaches

The Middle Reaches

Driving along the A40 between Oxford and Cheltenham I am always fascinated by the truly breathtaking view of the Windrush valley one has shortly before the turn to Burford: how motorists resist the temptation to turn off and explore is beyond me! This area has enough single track roads to satisfy the most inveterate snooper and even an indefatigable explorer such as myself finds something new each time one passes through. As mentioned in the foreword, tourists usually confine themselves to the market town of Burford and this amazes me as, beautiful though Burford is, there is so much in the surrounding countryside to enjoy if one can tear oneself away from the cosy tearooms on the High Street.

Having said that, Burford is undoubtedly the "star" of the area and is an essential visit. This is nothing new as, in the seventeenth century, horse races over the downs surrounding the town attracted as motley a crew as any one could find there today – including Charles II and Nell Gwynne, whose son was made the Earl of Burford. The church is well worth a visit and its size reflects the importance of the town in previous times: indeed, one of the stained glass windows was chosen to form a special Christmas postage stamp in recent years. Less happily, in 1649 some mutineers from Cromwell's Model Army were held in the church and three were executed against the church wall – not before one of them, Anthony Sedley left his mark for posterity through carving his name on the font. In a typically pragmatic country way in years gone by the truly enormous monuments in the churchyard were used as stores for poached livestock taken from the old Wychwood Forest, the remnants of which may be found on the hills above the town. Presumably the poachers asked the incumbents' permission first!

Staying on less than savoury topics, the nearby village of Fulbrook was home, not of Dirty Harry, but of Tom, Dick and Harry, brothers who terrorised the surrounding neighbourhood and whose careers in crime included raiding the Oxford-Gloucester coach. Their reign of terror came to an end when their plot to rob one of the local manors was foiled by the local constabulary: Dick was never seen again after severing his own arm to escape from the police but Tom and Harry were hanged at Gloucester.

Another famous (or infamous) set of siblings came from Swinbrook: the Mitford sisters, who lived at Swinbrook House when they were children. Two of them, Nancy (the author of *The Pursuit of Love*) and Unity are buried in the churchyard of St Mary's, Swinbrook. This church also houses the truly extravagant tombs of the Fettiplace family which are a monument to their egos if nothing else! Unfortunately nothing remains of their house, although standing in the churchyard and looking down to the river one can see the remains of their fishponds.

The walks around this area are some of my favourites and are interesting even in the winter, although wellingtons are advised owing to the large amounts of mud one can encounter. I usually start from Burford and follow the footpaths up the hill to Fulbrook and across the fields to a patch of forest. Following the path down a long ride, one reaches the "deserted" village of Widford and what is called locally "the church in the fields". This is the tiny chapel of St Oswald which used to be surrounded by the usual collection of cottages but which stands now entirely on its own in the middle of a field; the only remnants of the old dwellings being the bumps left in the ground around the graveyard. During restoration of the church earlier this century it was discovered that it lies on top of a Roman mosaic, indicating the presence of the remains of a substantial villa. Unfortunately there are not funds at present to investigate any further so this is one "secret" which remains to be discovered!

From Widford move eastwards and thus to Swinbrook Church and the village of Swinbrook. I recommend a visit to The Swan, a cosy hostelry perched on the bank of the Windrush, particularly welcome outside the summer months.for its log fire. From the Swan continue eastwards along the banks of the river to Asthall Leigh and another of my favourite pubs, the Maybush, which is an excellent place to eat. At this point the walker has a choice, to turn and follow the gentle meanderings of the Windrush back to Burford or to continue up the steep rise to the A40 using the remains of the old Roman road Akerman Street. If the latter course is followed, it is necessary to cross the A40 and follow the various footpaths and single track roads to the village of Shilton.

Shilton used to have a Cistercian priory snd you can still see the monks' dovecote on the left as you enter the village. On an even more picturesque note, the steep descent into the village culminates in a ford which looks as if it came straight from a Constable painting. On a hot day it is delightful to sit in the shade of the enormous tree bordering this spot and watch the village children playing in the ford – probably much as their ancestors have done for hundreds of years. Climb the steep slope on the other side of the ford and turn right. If you keep going you will reach Burford again and will have earned a visit to one of the many excellent tea shops - I am especially fond of the Burford House Hotel which I believe has the most comfortable sofas in Oxfordshire.

The above is only one example of walks one can undertake in the area and even a cursory glance at an Ordnance Survey map will suggest more than anybody could reasonably expect to choose from. Like a Chinese feast one is spoilt for choice and you will doubtless find your own secrets as soon as you begin to explore.

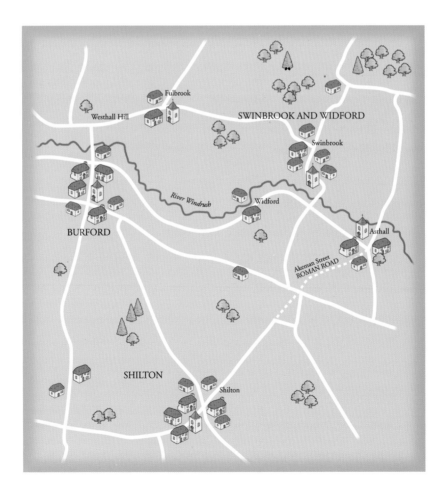

The Cottage

This has a very simple title because it is simply the typical dream cottage. I have been entirely captivated by its charms and I hope that you will be too! This design is based on the appearance of the building in summer when all the colourful flowers are at their best but it is equally as attractive in the winter time when the warmth of the Cotswold stone offsets the frosty landscape perfectly. This is definitely the cottage for all seasons!

Clue: Not full for long and an uphill struggle to bring home the bacon!

The Cottage

Page Layout:

51	52	53
54	55	56

illustration based on a detail from the engraving of a local gravestone

Key

Cross stitch in two strands

Stitch Count: 177 x 155

		DMC	Anchor
•	Light Stone	3033	387
←	Bright Grass Green	470	266
►	Dark Forest Green	895	269
⌐	Very Pale Sky	747	158
⊥	Mid Moss Green	937	368
⟍	Steel Grey	318	399
▽	Dark Pine Green	502	876
◤	Parrot Green	986	245
△	Rose Pink	224	894
★	Mid Golden-Brown	370	855
/	Mauve	552	100
⊞	Moss Green	936	846
◆	Honey	437	362
−	Pale Grey-Blue	928	847
⊘	Dark Stone	3032	392
X	Stone Grey	3022	1040
▲	Very Dark Moss Green	934	862

		DMC	Anchor
◇	Pale Honey	738	942
□	Mid Stone	3782	391
●	Very Dark Slate	3021	273
＼	Mint Green	3347	266
+	Light Forest Green	3346	257
⊡	Pale Mink	642	831
◊	Dove Grey	3023	832
↘	Very Light Stone	822	390
∧	Pale Mauve	553	98
ꝯ	Dark Rose Pink	223	895
✳	Light Steel Grey	415	398
M	Dark Grass Green	469	267
♡	Dark Mink	3790	393
▬	Dark Stone Brown	3781	1008
,	Dark Butter Yellow	3821	305
	White	Blanc	2
■	Black	310	403

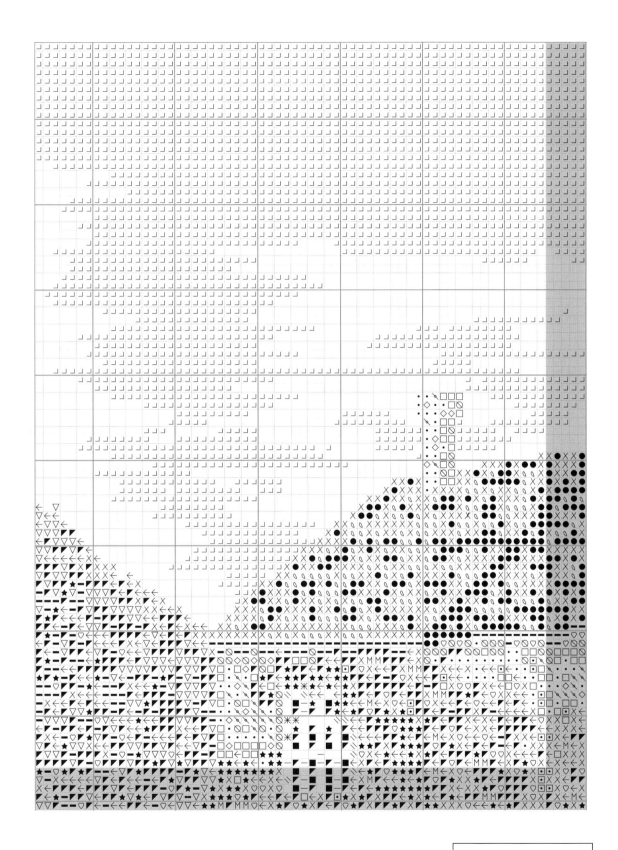

continued on p. 52

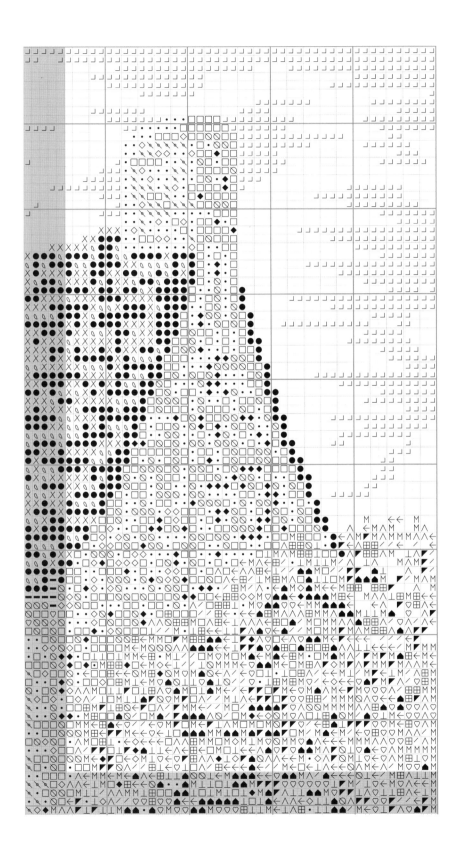

continued on p. 54

53 ❧

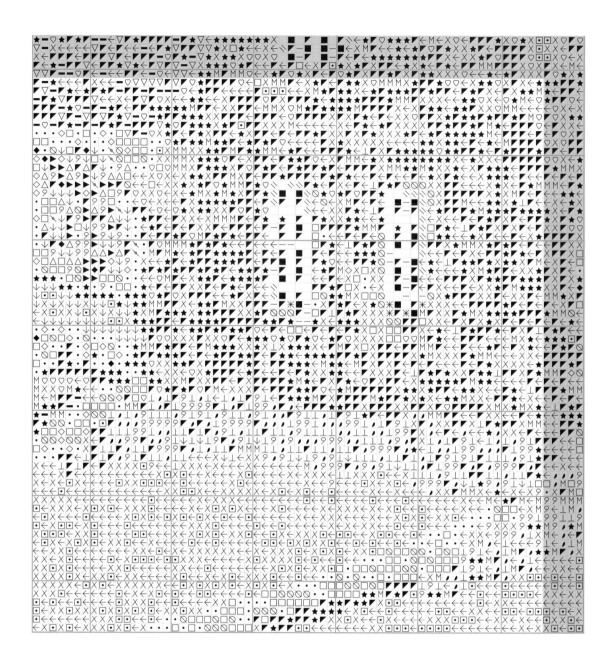

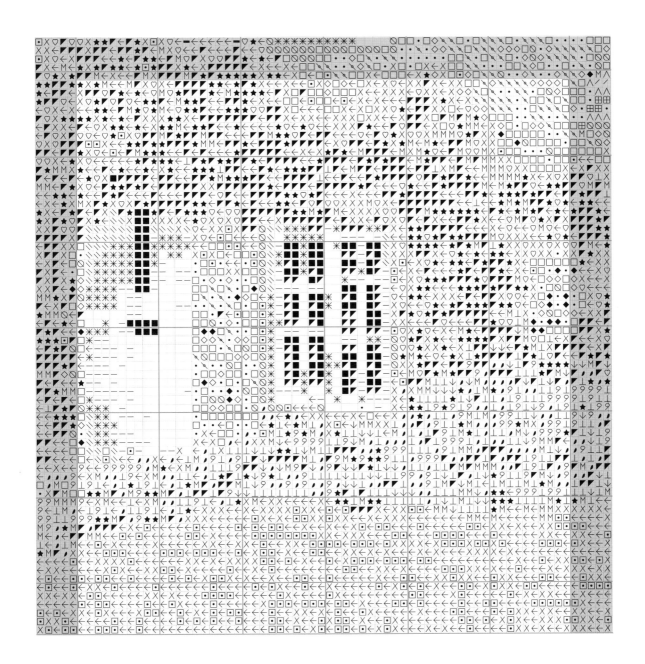

continued on p. 56

55

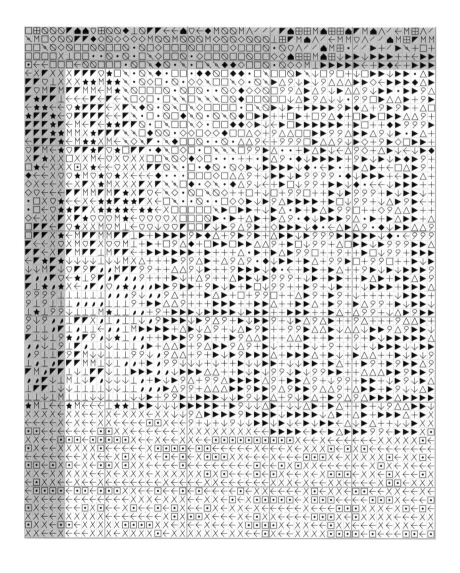

The Hotel

As the title suggests, this is in fact a hotel and reflects the flexibility with which the old buildings adapt to modern village life. Although I don't live far from here, at times I am sorely tempted to book myself in, if only for the joy of looking out of my bedroom window to see the profusion of flowers shown here. Even in wintertime one can imagine the comfy sofas and roaring log fires that must surely lie inside – and can you imagine anything more inviting than the open gateway at the end of the path?

Clue: Opposite the way to the village heart and the seat of its memories.

Key			
Cross stitch in two strands			
		DMC	Anchor
●	Very Dark Slate	3021	273
−	Light Grass Green	859	3052
▽	Light Blue-Grey	3072	234
○	Light Stone	3033	387
▪	Very Dark Rose Pink	3722	1027
＝	Dark Butter Yellow	3821	307
ˈˈ	Butter Yellow	3822	305
⊖	Dark Stone	3032	392
∴	Pale Sky	747	158
□	Mid Stone	3782	391
╱	Very Pale Grey	762	234
◇	Pale Honey	738	942
◥	Mid Beige	612	831
9	Dark Rose Pink	223	895
△	Rose Pink	224	894
✳	Violet	792	177
M	Dark Grass Green	469	267
◖	Mid Brown	611	832
▶	Dark Forest Green	895	269
▽	Pale Violet	3807	118
✓	Dove Grey	3023	832
←	Bright Grass Green	470	266
◉	Forest Green	3345	268
+	Light Forest Green	3346	257
⊠	Dark Chocolate Brown	3371	382
⊠	Dark Brown	610	889
◀	Chocolate Brown	938	381
▣	Dark Slate	3787	10
⊤	Slate	646	8581
	White	Blanc	2
■	Black	310	403
	Backstitch in two strands		
—	Black	310	403

The Hotel

Page Layout:

58	59
60	61
62	63

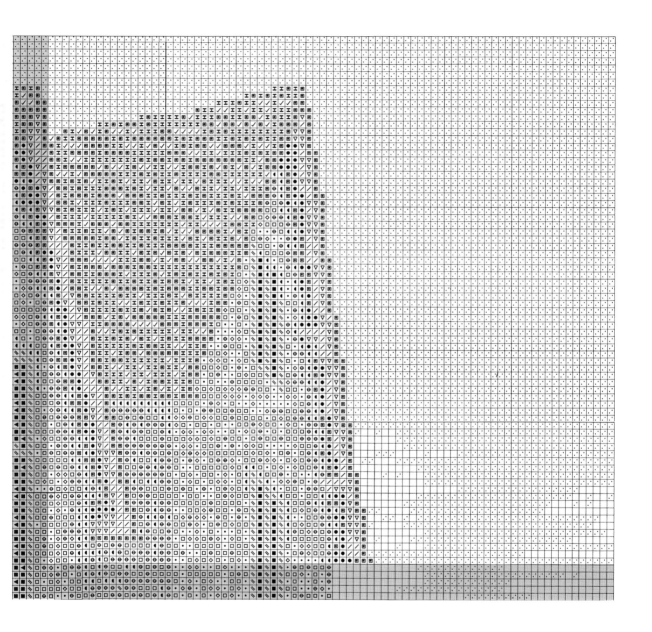

continued on p. 60

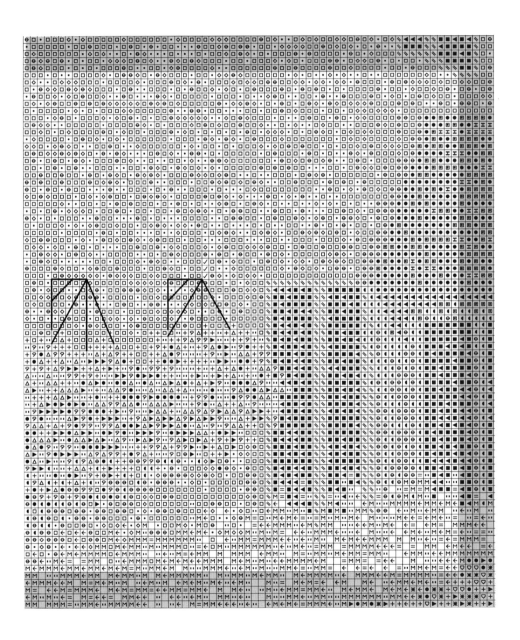

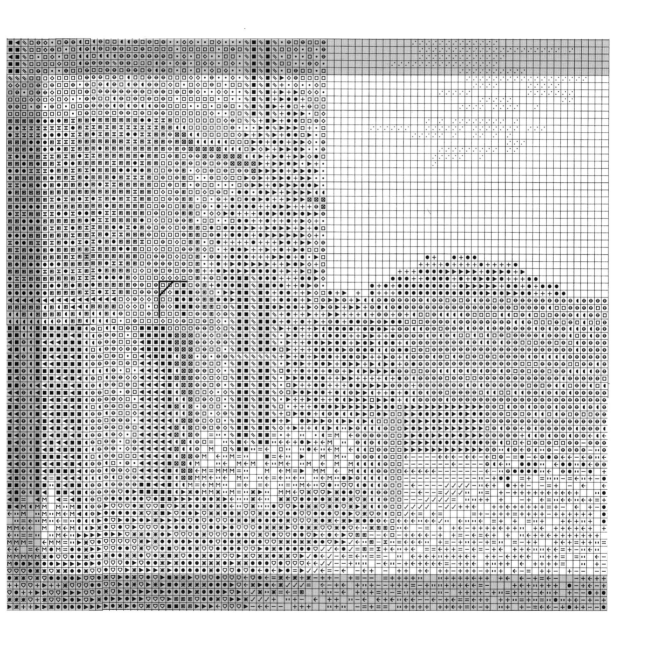

continued on p. 62

The Hotel

continued from p. 61

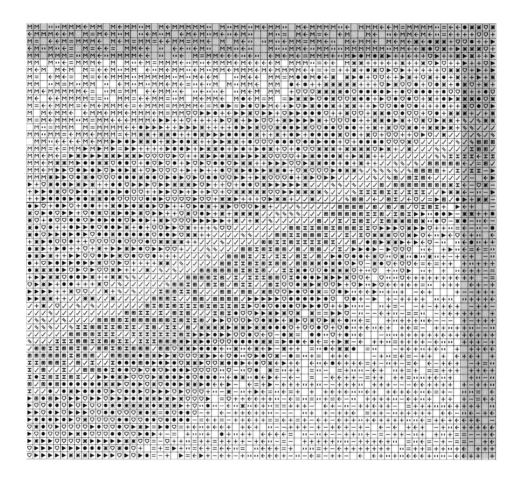

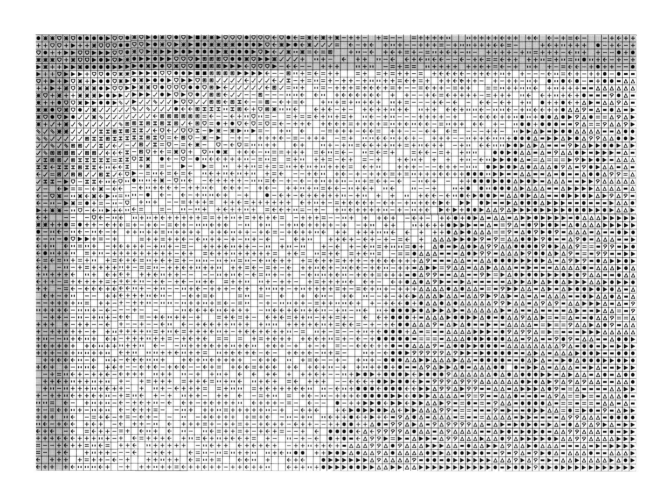

The Invitation

At first glance this seems a strange title for this design but I am sure you will agree that the steps invite one to climb up and see what they lead to – and to examine the extraordinary lamp which always reminds me of C S Lewis's Narnia series. This is obviously an autumn picture as I find the combination of red berries and fallen leaves entirely irresistible but I was hard pushed to withstand the appeal of springtime when the bank is covered with a carpet of snowdrops and the first early daffodils. Although I am usually pushed for time when passing this spot I am always tempted to stop and walk up the steps and I always notice something different when I succumb – perhaps an unusual fungus hiding in the step corners or winter revealing a bird's nest tucked away deep in the tree. I hope you will take up the invitation!

Clue: Gateway to the haunt of the famous, the infamous and the forgotten.

Page Layout:

65	66
67	68

Stitch Count: 120 x 159

Key

Cross stitch in two strands

		DMC	Anchor
✳	Light Forest Green	3346	257
⊠	Dark Brown	610	889
⊞	Very Dark Slate	3021	273
▶	Dark Forest Green	895	269
▼	Dark Mink	3790	393
ⲭ	Forest Green	3345	268
—	Very Pale Grey	762	234
⊘	Dark Stone	3032	392
✕	Dark Steel Grey	414	235
◁	Dark Green-Gold	731	281
−	Moss Green	936	846
T	Pale Grey	415	398
⋈	Blood Red	814	44
◪	Berry Red	816	43
◣	Light Olive	732	281
▲	Very Dark Moss Green	934	862
◢	Pond Green	3051	860
	White	Blanc	2
→	Mid Moss Green	937	268
◇	Pale Honey	738	942
·	Cold Sky	827	976
☐	Mid Stone	3782	391
⊡	Pale Mink	642	831
●	Dark Moss Green	935	263
♥	Mid Brown	611	832
○	Steel Grey	318	399
⌐	Pale Sky	828	975
■	Black	310	403

Backstitch in two strands

—	Black	310	403

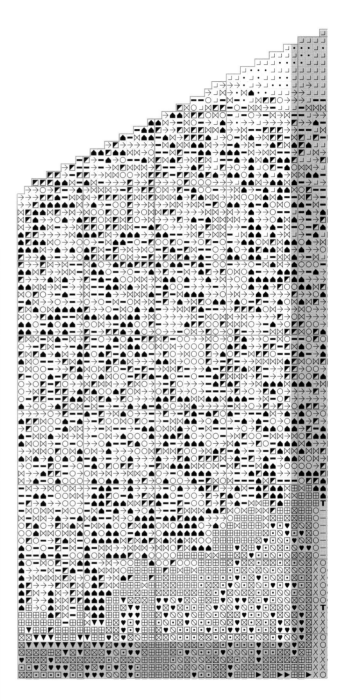

continued on p. 66

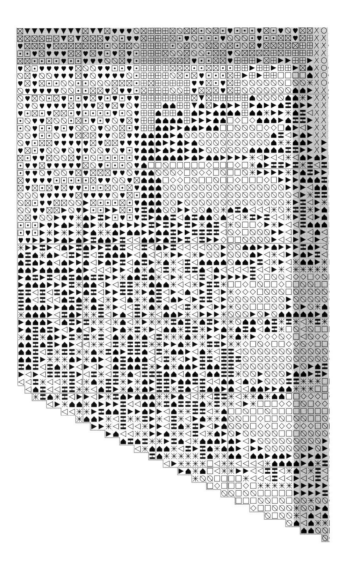

continued on p. 68

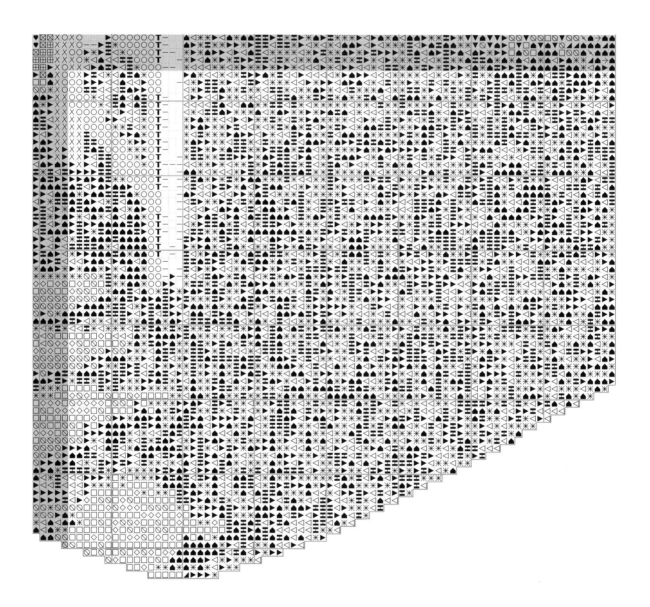

Spring Churchyard

It is quite obvious what this design is of and I am not going to make the precise location any easier to find by giving away any clues! Suffice it to say that this is everything I think a village church should be. This design was one of many I could have drawn from this wonderful building but as I have a particular fondness for daffodils it had an unfair advantage from the start. Furthermore, the fact that I could include the ivy clad stone wall in the foreground I feel "raises" the building and increases the sense of discovery I try to inject into all my designs. The church, however, remains somehow comfortable and approachable probably due again to the wonderful warm quality of the stonework or perhaps the sense of the balmy summer to come?

Spring Churchyard

Page Layout:

70	**71**	**72**
73	**74**	**75**

Stitch Count: 176 x 107

Key

Cross stitch in two strands

		DMC	Anchor
\	Daffodil Yellow	743	302
	White	Blanc	2
⊠	Dark Brown	610	889
⌐	Pale Sky	3753	1031
⊡	Dark Slate	3787	10
◢	Light Charcoal	645	8581
•	Light Stone	3033	387
⬟	Very Dark Moss Green	934	862
P	Mid Stone	3782	391
◇	Pale Honey	738	942
↖	Mid Brown	611	832
▬	Moss Green	936	846
—	Cream	822	390
★	Very Dark Slate	3021	273
●	Dark Moss Green	935	263
X	Slate	3022	1040
M	Dark Grass Green	469	267
⁄	Mint Green	3347	266
✳	Light Forest Green	3346	257
⊥	Mid Moss Green	937	268
⊘	Dark Stone	3032	392
■	Black	310	403

Backstitch in two strands

—	Dark Stone	3032	392

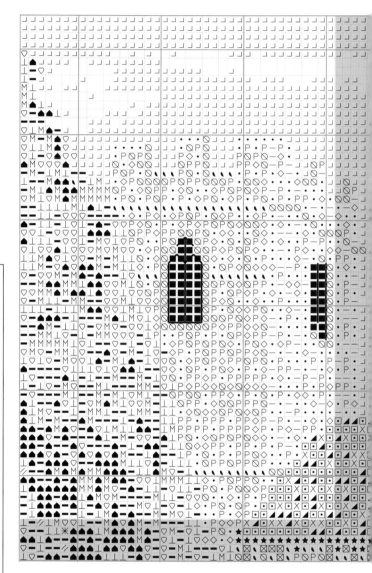

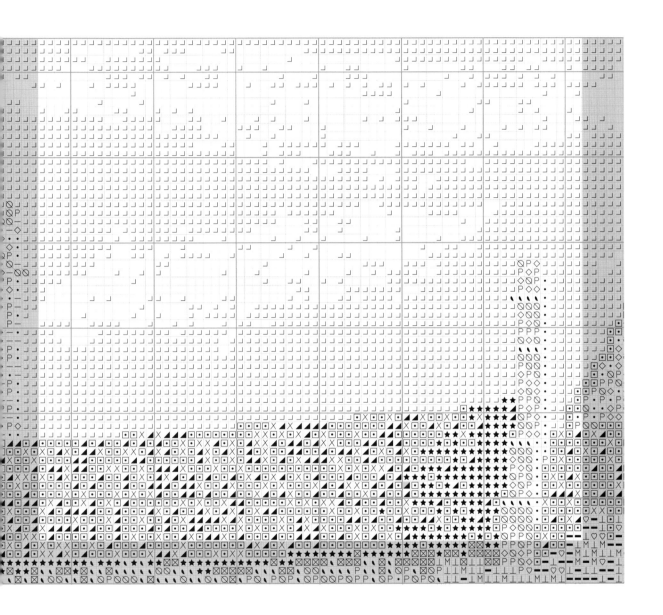

continued on p. 72

Spring Churchyard
continued from p. 71

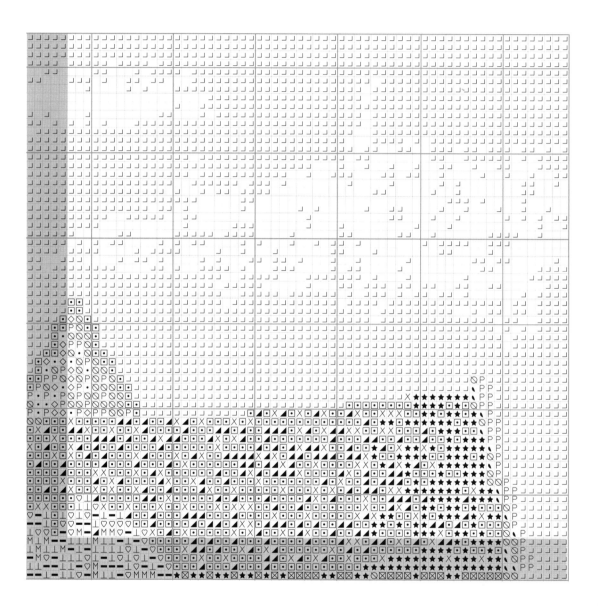

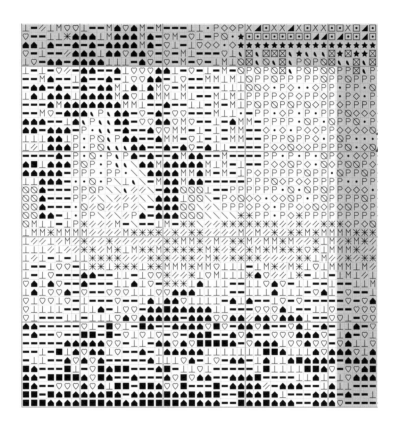

continued on p.74

Classical Gate

I must admit that this is the design which I have altered most from real life, not in terms of the gate itself or the fascinating topiary but with regard to their surroundings. Therefore it is quite difficult to discover its secret and I will be very impressed if anybody manages it! I felt that somehow the hard shape of the gate contrasted wonderfully with the soft topiary outline and their colours also diverged, creating a classical restful feel not unlike an architectural drawing. However, the question remains: what is the gateway the entrance to?

Clue: Climb every mountain; ford every stream.

Page Layout:

78	79

Key

Cross stitch in two strands

Stitch Count: 176 x 107

		DMC	Anchor			DMC	Anchor
−	Dark Brown	610	889	◄	Dark Willow	520	861
↖	Mink	640	832	＼	Willow	522	859
■	Dark Forest Green	895	269	·	Pale Willow	523	858
◢	Forest Green	3345	268	T	Mid Moss Green	937	268
▽	Dark Stone	3032	392	=	Pale Honey	738	942
☆	Moss Green	936	846	⊡	Pond Green	3051	860
⋈	Dark Slate	3787	10	✓	Mid Brown	611	832
◆	Mid Beige	612	831	＼	Light Stone-Grey	644	830
♡	Mid Stone	3782	391	⊘	Light Beige	613	853
⊥	Light Forest Green	3346	257	⊞	Pale Mink	642	831
−	Mint Green	3347	266	○	Light Stone	3033	387
⌐	Pale Sky	747	158	□	White	Blanc	2

		DMC	Anchor
—	*Backstitch in two strands*		
	Black	310	403

Classical Gate

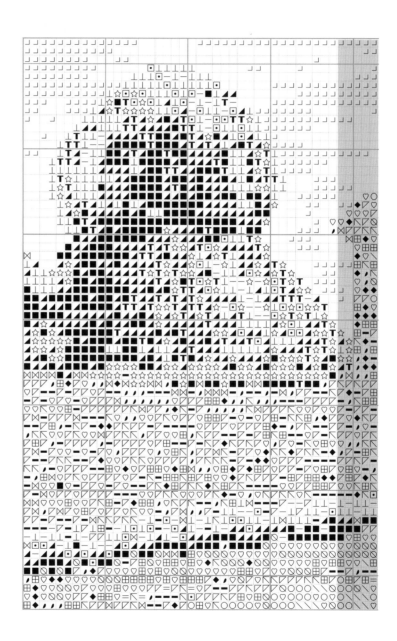

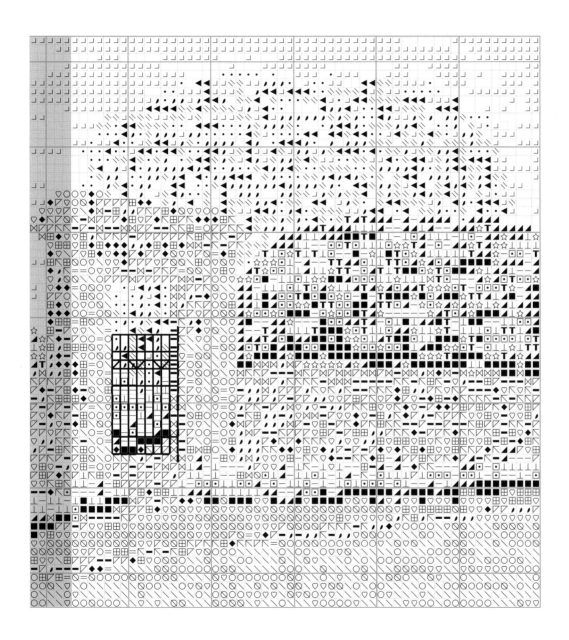

Part 3

The Lower Windrush Valley

The Lower Windrush Valley

Although not actually in the official Cotswolds Area of Outstanding Natural Beauty, I do not think it is fair to regard the lower Windrush region as "filler" between Oxford and the Cotswolds proper. At the time of writing the English Tourist Board agree with me and include this area in its section on the Cotswolds although, being awkward, I am not entirely happy with this either as personally I think this area combines the best attributes of both Oxford and the wider Cotswolds and should be given a category all of its own!

There is certainly much for the traveller to admire, particularly outside the main A40-A415 corridors. In particular I would mention the many mills which flourish on the banks of the Windrush – tribute to the old wool trade – some of which have open days throughout the year. There are also vineyards to keep the wine-buffs amused and the Farm Museum at Cogges is not to be missed. Steven Baughan's pottery at Aston produces pottery which combines the best of country traditions – pieces which are both functional, beautiful and good value. For the engineers, a visit to Filkins is a necessity, not only to enjoy the atmosphere of this tiny village, but also to be amazed that the ancient machinery at the mill is still capable of functioning, let alone producing the beautiful soft shades of wool which can be bought at truly bargain prices. Finally, for anybody like me who finds cakes and pastries totally irresistible, the baker's shop in Lechlade sells doughnuts which are everything a doughnut should be – filled with far too much jam and smothered in sugar!

As far as walks are concerned, both of the ones I regularly embark upon begin in Standlake (where one has a choice of two pubs from which to start!). **Warning:** for the first one you should take a towel as you have to cross a ford – I was certainly caught out the first time I went this way. From Standlake, head past the Mulberry Bush school across the fields towards Old Shifford. Past the farm you will find the ford – which is lovely to cross on a really hot day – and you should head towards Shifford Lock on the Thames. I have spent hours here, especially in the summer, just watching the variety of boats passing through and the different reactions of the people steering them into the lock. Cross the Thames and follow the river downstream on its southern bank. On this stretch it doesn't matter what time of year it is as there is always something to see, ranging from the wildlife (swans, ducks and kingfishers being just a few) to the pitcher plants in the woods bordering the river. On reaching Newbridge, where the Windrush joins the Thames, one is spoilt for choice in terms of pubs as there are two – you can even take a break from walking and hire a punt from the Maybush in the summer time. Alternatively there is often live jazz at either that pub or the Rose Revived – what could be more relaxing on a hot Sunday afternoon? To return to Standlake you can either follow the A415 back to the village or walk across the fields towards Cow Lane which takes you back into Standlake village along Rack End.

The second walk also begins in Standlake but from Church End. Cross the Windrush and head out past the lakes towards Stanton Harcourt. You will have to cross and recross the river several times – see if you catch sight of the heron! This is one of my favourite stretches of the river (at this point split in two) and you always see some fish speeding up and down. On reaching Stanton Harcourt I recommend a visit to the Harcourt Arms which is particularly cosy in wintertime owing to the log fires and comfy sofas. If you can bear to drag yourself away, head towards Bablockhythe where there is another pub to keep your spirits up! Until fairly recently there used to be a ferry operating between the pub bank and that opposite and you can still see the now sadly redundant ferry boat which is moored close to the pub. Follow the Thames westward and you will come to Northmoor lock, which like its counterpart at Shifford, is a good place to watch the world go by. If you are as nosy as I am you will be fascinated by the variety of dwellings which have been put up on the opposite bank which, however, do not seem to interfere with the wildlife as I usually see at least two muntjack deer every time I walk this way. Eventually you will reach Newbridge and the Maybush/Rose Revived and you can return to Standlake via either of the two ways mentioned above.

I think it is fair to tell you the four designs from this area are taken from Standlake and Stanton Harcourt. Unfortunately the former village has suffered from inappropriate infilling but it is still worth visiting if only to see the variety of architectural styles present in such a small area – ranging from typical solid Cotswold stone farmhouses, to imposing Elizabethan half timbered structures, to "chocolate-box" thatched cottages. St Giles Church is particularly interesting as it has an unusual hexagonal tower and there is also a charming little brick Methodist chapel. Despite (or perhaps because of) this appearance of godliness, legend has it that in the sixteenth century Standlake had the highest percentage of witches per capita of anywhere in the country (some would argue they are still there!).

In contrast Stanton Harcourt boasts the shrine of St Edburg which may be found in the parish church of St Michael. Stanton Harcourt Manor, the seat of Earl Harcourt's family, is open to the public on various days throughout the summer and is well worth a visit if only for the excellent teas served by the village ladies in the ancient Old Kitchen! (Alexander) Pope's Tower stands in the grounds and the tiny domestic chapel, stew ponds and gardens are delightfully peaceful even when thronging with excited visitors.

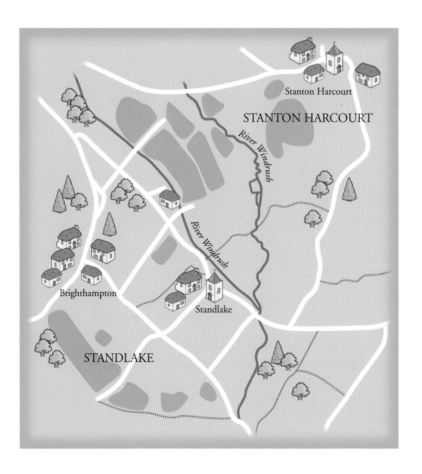

Autumn Barn

I guarantee this will frustrate even the most avid sniffer-out of secrets as it is indeed very hard to find! In fairness, the design is based on the appearance of the barn in autumn when the Russian vine, lavender and honeysuckle berries are at their best and when the roses are just giving their last blooms: it looks very different in springtime where the avid lady-gardener who tends this plot has created a true feast for the eyes.

Clue: Perched between and ancient and modern, you have to look beyond the gate.

Autumn Barn

Page Layout:

87	**88**

Stitch Count: 100 x 83

Key

Cross stitch in two strands

		DMC	Anchor			DMC	Anchor
◣	Very Dark Moss Green	934	862	⊥	Mid Moss Green	937	268
▽	Grey	647	397	M	Dark Grass Green	469	267
⌐	Pale Sky	747	158	✳	Light Forest Green	3346	257
⊡	Dark Slate	3787	10	◣	Dark Chocolate Brown	3371	382
◸	Pale Terracotta	3828	373	▽	Dark Red	815	1005
/	Straw	739	1009	−	Ecru	Ecru	926
○	Light Stone	3033	387	≡	Cherry Red	498	1006
⊘	Dark Stone	3032	392	//	Mint Green	3347	266
□	Mid Stone	3782	391	☆	Stone Grey	3022	1040
⅃	Pale Honey	738	942	Ⅵ	Light Green-Grey	368	214
△	Light Olive	732	281	|	Jade Green	320	215
━	Mid Green-Grey	367	216	8	Warm Chocolate Brown	898	340
△	Rose Pink	224	894	★	Mid Brown	611	832
←	Pale Green-Gold	733	280	⟍	Mid Beige	612	831
▶	Moss Green	936	846	◢	Pale Lavender	3042	870
⬚	Dark Rose Pink	223	895	◪	Lavender	3041	871

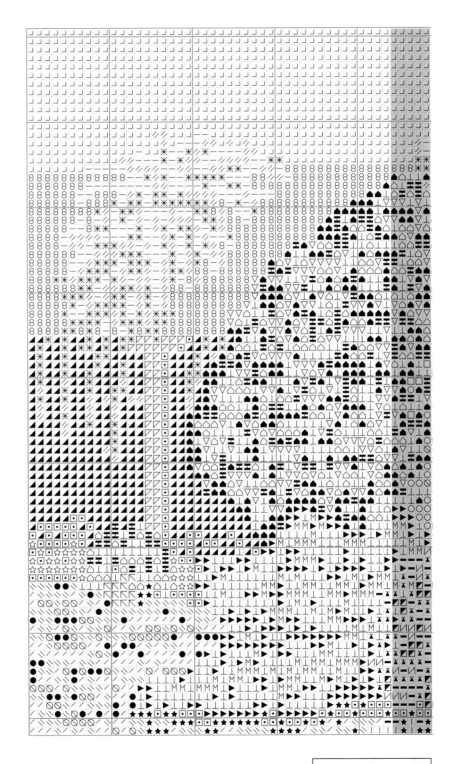

continued on p. 88

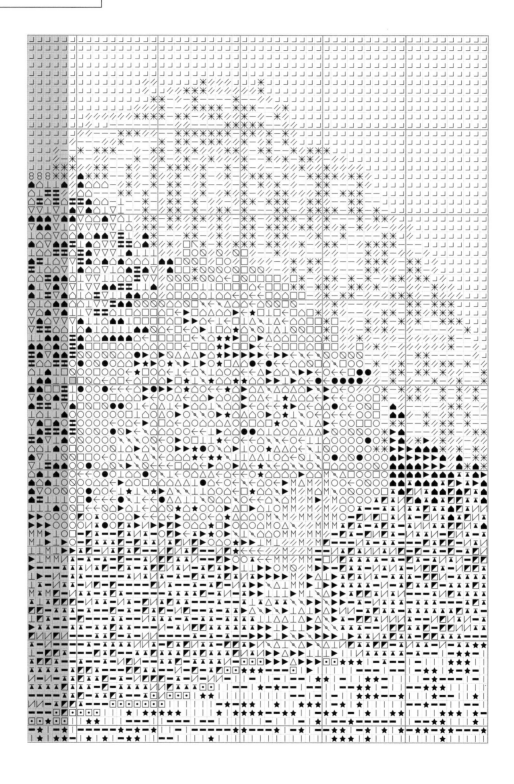

Honeysuckle Cottage

This is not the name of the cottage, but rather reflects the wonderful scent of honeysuckle mingling with lavender which one can enjoy when passing on warm summer nights. Actually the name of the cottage is rather surprising and known only to the initiated few! The cottage itself is unusual in that it is faced in brick rather than stone – providing variety for the architectural observer. I particularly enjoy the contrast this produces with the Cotswold stone wall, which is one of the few left in the village and much treasured as a result.

Clue: May not be found in Church or High but rather on the shelf.

Honeysuckle Cottage

Page Layout:

91	**92**
94	**95**

Stitch Count: 100 x 103

Key
Cross stitch in two strands

		DMC	Anchor
□	Mid Stone	3782	391
⃠	Dark Stone	3032	392
T	Warm Chocolate Brown	898	360
◇	Pale Honey	738	942
★	Mid Brown	611	832
✳	Light Forest Green	3346	257
⁄	Mint Green	3347	266
⊑	Forest Green	3345	268
⊠	Dark Brick	300	352
⊥	Mid Moss Green	937	268
✐	Very Dark Moss Green	934	862
M	Dark Grass Green	469	267
▬	Moss Green	936	846
△	Dusky Pink	316	60
●	Dark Dusky Pink	3726	1018
=	Honeysuckle	3822	305
↓	Golden Yellow	3820	307
⊞	Amber	433	371
↘	Mid Golden-Brown	370	855
⊠	Chocolate Brown	938	381
⌐	Light Blue-Grey	3072	234
◪	Amber Brown	801	359
♥	Light Amber	434	365
	White	Blanc	2
■	Black	310	403

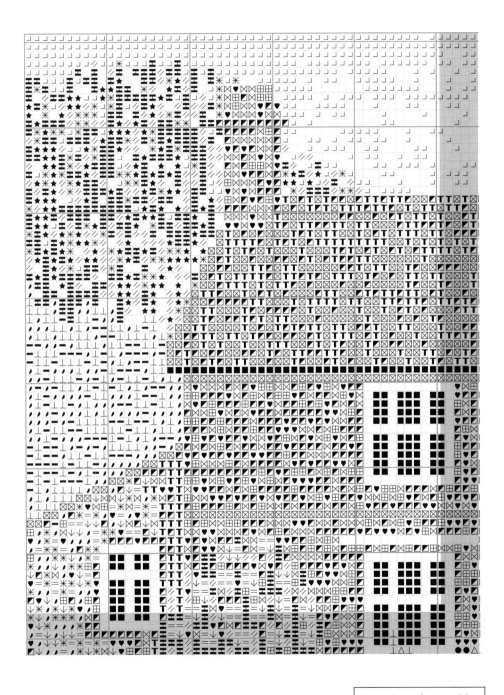

continued on p.92

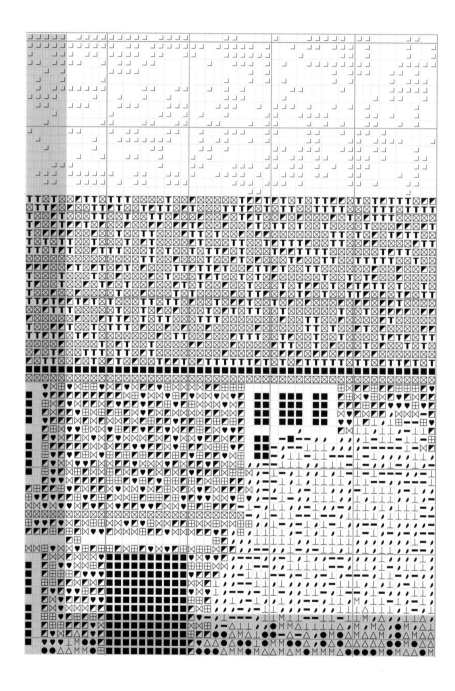

continued on p. 94

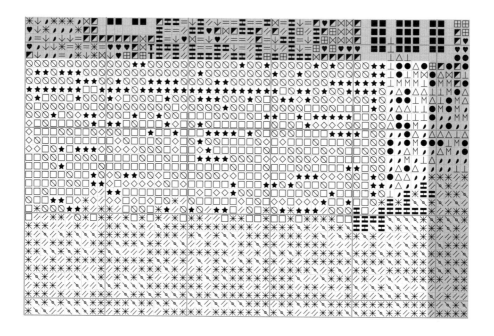

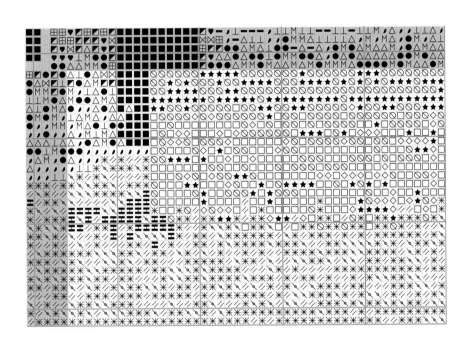

The Tradesman's Entrance

This is the easiest design to track down as there are few places grand enough to boast a tradesman's entrance displaying this degree of size and elegance. I particularly enjoy the clean classical lines and simple, clean detailing above the door.

Clue: Moving from the earthly to the spiritual, along the pilgrims' way?

Page Layout:

97	**98**
99	**100**

Stitch Count: 100 x 135

Key

Cross stitch in two strands

		DMC	Anchor
■	Black	310	403
•	Pale Grey	415	398
◇	Very Pale Grey	762	234
□	White	Blanc	2
Y	Dark Slate	3787	10
◀	Mink	640	832
T	Mid Stone	3782	391
/	Light Stone	3033	387
◁	Pale Honey	738	942
H	Very Light Stone	822	390
∪	Warm Chocolate Brown	898	360
✕	Dark Brown Stone	3781	1008
P	Slate	3022	1040
●	Dove Grey	3023	832
⌐	Sky	3761	160
∃	Dark Brown	610	889
F	Very Dark Moss Green	934	862
◆	Moss Green	936	846
♥	Mid Moss Green	937	268
N	Forest Green	3345	268
⊞	Light Forest Green	3346	257
∷	Dark Stone	3032	392
╲	Mid Brown	611	832

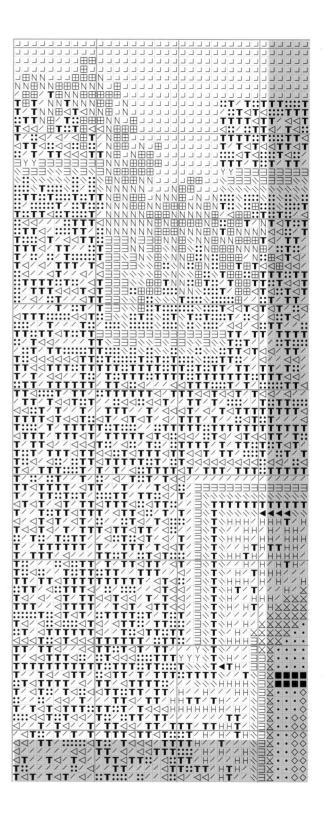

continued on p. 98

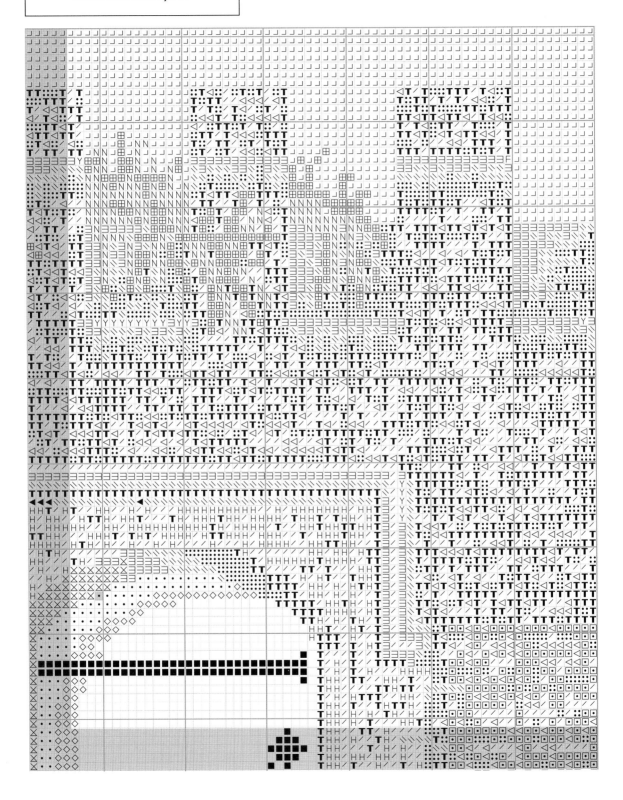

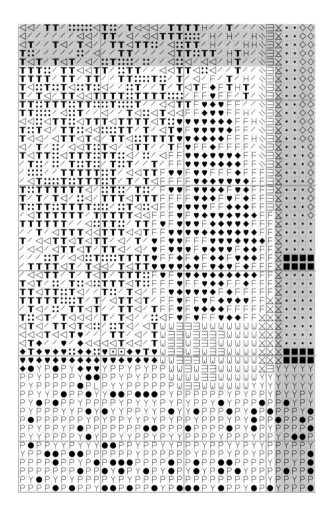

continued on p. 100

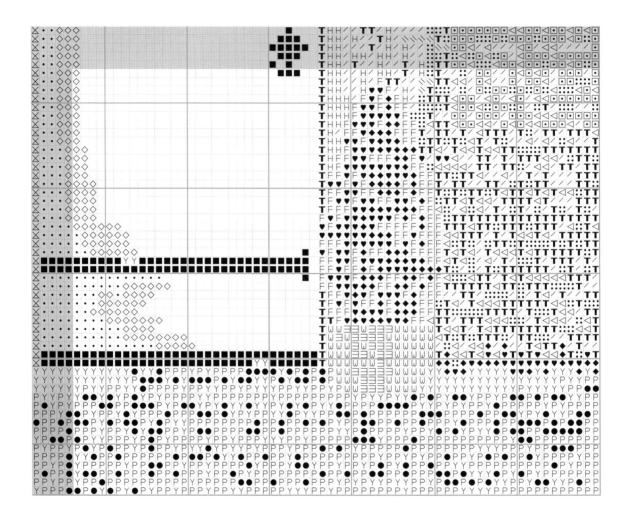

The Chimneys

This is another relatively easy design to trace so no prizes for finding it! I pass this cottage almost every time I go into Oxford and am continually amazed by the skill and ingenuity of the owners in filling their hanging baskets and window boxes with colour all the year round This is really my thank-you to them for cheering me up with their imagination even on the most adverse gloomy February days, although I might add that they do have competition from the cottage over the road!

Clue: Gateway tothe village?

The Chimneys

Page Layout:

102	103	104
106	107	108

Stitch Count: 120 x 118

Key

Cross stitch in two strands

		DMC	Anchor
⊞	Amber	433	371
⋈	Light Amber	434	365
M	Dark Grass Green	469	267
◪	Amber Brown	801	359
		Very Light Stone Pink	543	933
▽	Light Stone Pink	842	376
⊡	Chocolate Brown	938	381
✕	Mid Stone Pink	841	378
—	Cream	822	390
▽	Grass Green	470	266
◢	Warm Chocolate Brown	898	360
△	Rose Pink	224	894
T	Raspberry	3722	1027
●	Dark Stone Pink	840	379
⌐	Mid Brown	611	832
◁	Dark Brown Stone	3781	1008
⊘	Dark Stone	3032	392
◆	Dark Golden-Brown	830	277
✳	Light Forest Green	3346	257
♡	Cinnamon	869	906
━	Moss Green	936	846
⊥	Mid Moss Green	937	268
⌐	Pale Sky	747	158
⊟	Butter Yellow	3822	305
⬟	Golden Yellow	3820	307
∥	Mint Green	3347	266
╱	Lettuce Green	3348	253
⚏	Forest Green	3362	269
=	Light Forest Green	3363	262
▼	Very Dark Brown Stone	3031	905
⊠	Dark Brown	610	889
☐	Mid Stone	3782	391
⋈	Dark Brick	300	352
	White	Blanc	2
■	Black	310	403

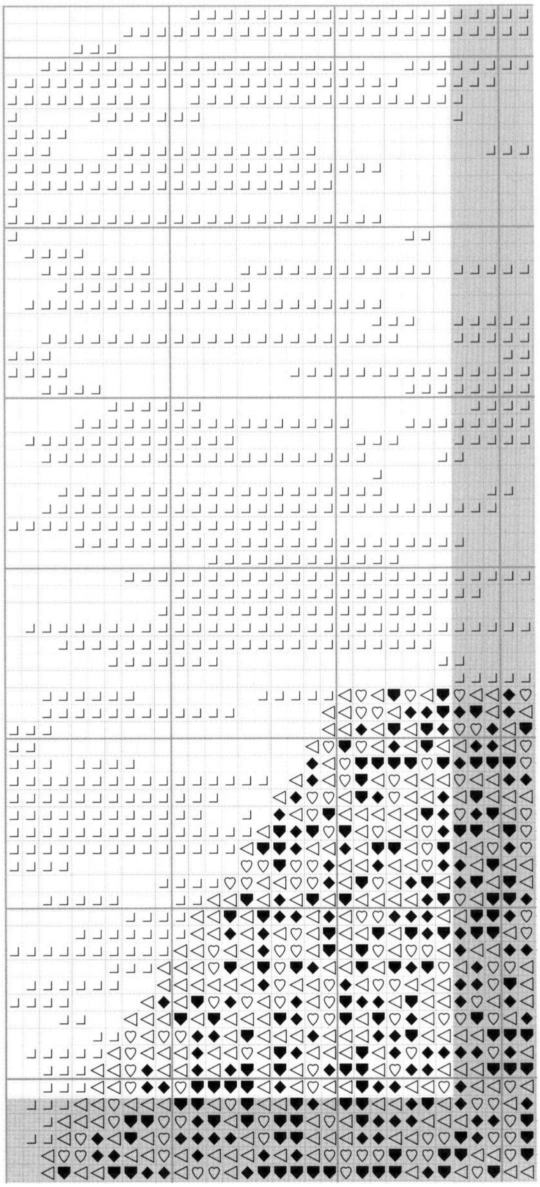

102

continued on p. 104

continued on p. 106

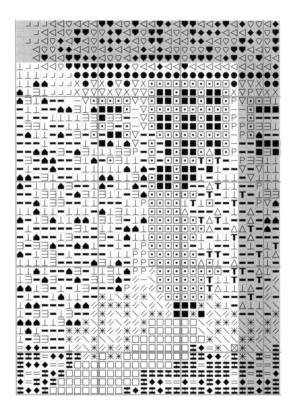

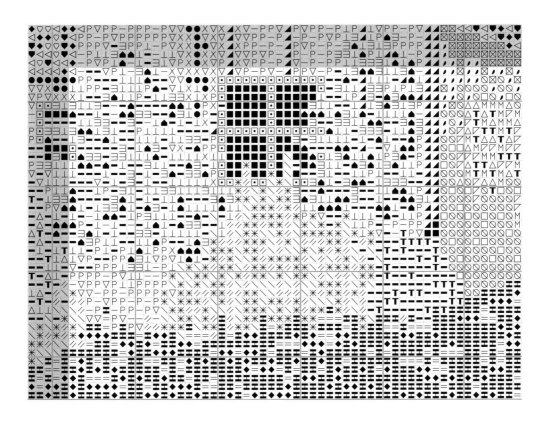

continued on p. 108

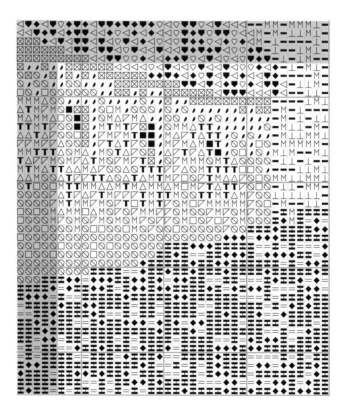

Cross Stitch Titles

from the Black Sheep Press

If you have enjoyed this book, please look out for future titles in the 'Secret England' series, including 'Secret Cornwall' & 'Secret Highlands', as well as a book of traditional samplers, all available soon from the Black Sheep Press.

The Black Sheep Press of Oxford Ltd

P.O. Box 722, Oxford OX2 6XR

Notes

Notes